Interior Landmarks
Treasures of New York

Interior Landmarks
Treasures of New York

Judith Gura and Kate Wood

Foreword by Hugh Hardy

Afterword by Barbaralee Diamonstein-Spielvogel

Principal photography by Larry Lederman

The New York School of Interior Design

The Monacelli Press

Library of Congress Control Number: 2015938285
ISBN: 9781580934220
Designed by Yve Ludwig

Printed in China

The Monacelli Press
236 West 27th Street
New York, New York 10001
www.monacellipress.com

Foreword

Hugh Hardy

This is a city whose mythology has always been intimately associated with change. "What's new?" is intrinsically woven into the culture of the place, ours having traditionally been thought of as an urban center built to discover the latest novelty, be it in design ideas, ways to live, or how to make money. Celebration of the New York City Landmark Preservation Commission's fifty years of accomplishment therefore represents an astonishing achievement.

To date the commission has designated 117 public interiors as landmarks, and 47 are presented here. In order to strengthen the list of impending designations, our hope is that this publication will bring new awareness of the subject, confirming the wisdom of saving these designs and increasing public interest in what has been missed. The commission must continue to reinforce the idea that landmarks throughout all five boroughs have lasting value. In anticipation of the next fifty years of this goal, we also suggest that more careful consideration should be given before designation to how changes in the use of landmark interiors can be appropriately accommodated.

Although preservation of the exterior configuration of significant buildings has often been difficult to justify in a city so vigorously shaped by change, designated structures have periodically been adapted for radically different activities. Although these landmarks were saved because of their exterior appearance, startling interior alterations have been accepted by the commission without comment. Interiors present unique challenges. Each interior design was created for activities appropriate to its era. If designation restricted all changes in use, the value of the property to its owner could be significantly reduced, and public support for the designation process would be lost. Therefore, interpreting "appropriate" change is inherent in designating interiors, often requiring enlightened compromise.

Radio City Music Hall

A different dilemma confronts the commission when considering the vocabulary of modernism. The majority of building designations to date show a dedication to the masonry tradition. These are structures with thick walls that allow outside and inside to be responsive to different physical needs and governed by different design principles. In some nineteenth-century examples, the two have been deliberately contrasted with one another, offering a sequence of surprise and discovery. Modern structures, however, often assume outside and inside are one, with designs calculated to show no visual separation between the two.

This book records the rich legacy of design and historic associations we have inherited. Although the examples shown here all clearly deserve designation, what new work should now join them? By proposing new examples, the public can continue to help the commission consider what interiors are missing. When considering the vaunted diversity and energy of New York, we expect this process to be embellished with vibrant legacy. Now it is up to us.

Introduction

Judith Gura and Kate Wood

This book grew out of the exhibition "Rescued, Restored, Reimagined: New York's Landmark Interiors" at the New York School of Interior Design. Organized in conjunction with the citywide celebration of the fiftieth anniversary of the New York City Landmarks Law, the show—like this book—was the first ever to focus specifically on this city's landmark interiors.

What constitutes an interior landmark? It is a space determined by the Landmarks Preservation Commission (LPC) to have "special historical or aesthetic interest or value as part of the development, heritage or cultural characteristics of the city, state or nation." It must be "customarily open or accessible to the public, or to which the public is customarily invited"; it may, therefore, not be a private residence or, for constitutional reasons, a place of worship. And, like all landmark buildings, it must be at least thirty years old. Unfortunately, many interiors are remodeled or destroyed before they are eligible for designation.

In the late 1970s, the American Society of Interior Designers conducted a Survey of Significant Interiors, coordinated by R. Michael Brown, the only interior designer ever to serve on the LPC. The survey identified more than 700 New York interiors as worthy of designation, yet as of this writing, some thirty-five years later, there are only 117 interior landmarks. This is a startling disparity in view of the fact that, although buildings are principal contributors to the urban fabric, interiors are where we spend most of our time. They are the spaces in which New Yorkers work, learn, govern, dine, are entertained, and interact with their communities. Reflecting changing taste and documenting the diversity of the city's history, New York's public interiors are uniquely valuable.

Why, then, have so few been designated? Part of the problem lies with the complex nature of interiors themselves. Interiors are designed to be used, to meet the needs of a particular time, place, and purpose. They are flexible rather than fixed. People walk on their floors, sit in their seats, lean against their walls, touch the decorations, pull the handles. As daily wear and tear takes its toll, walls and ceilings must be periodically repainted, worn carpet and textiles replaced, broken or lost parts substituted, and furniture refinished, reupholstered or exchanged (though movable furnishings are not included in landmark designation). Interiors must keep pace with the evolving needs of those who use them.

Beyond that, improvements in lighting and climate control, legally mandated adaptations for visitor accessibility, or security issues may require alterations, sometimes costly and often time-consuming, that their designers never anticipated. If interiors are continually changing, how then can they remain as they were first intended? That is the challenge faced by preservationists: to balance past and present by maintaining, repairing, and restoring significant buildings and interiors without losing the integrity of the original designs.

Alterations to designated landmarks must be reviewed and approved by LPC. It is not surprising, then, that owners and operators have often opposed designation, resisting additional property controls. The premise of the law, however, is that landmark protection "is a public necessity and is required in the interest of the health, prosperity, safety and welfare of the people." The theaters, office building lobbies, and tourist destinations in this book are testimony to the importance of landmarks to New York's identity and economy.

Without the landmarks law, there would be no mechanism to prevent the destruction of such assets. The demolition of New York's Pennsylvania Station in 1963—a "monumental act of vandalism"—was the catalyst for the adoption of legislation that had been discussed in civic circles for many decades prior to 1965. Still, the original law was a very limited version of the much more robust legislation in place today. Though included in an early draft bill, interiors were left out of the original law because, as then-LPC Chair Harmon Goldstone explained, "we didn't want to bite off more than we could chew before we got established."

In her study "New York City Landmarks Preservation Commission (1962–1999): Paradigm for Changing Attitudes Toward Historic Preservation," Marjorie Pearson, LPC director of research from 1978 to 1999, provides a scholarly, first-hand account of the law's successes and failures during a large part of its first half-century, during which it emerged as a potentially powerful force in shaping the city. Several key moments related to interiors merit discussion here.

The old Metropolitan Opera house, torn down in 1967, two years after the landmarks law was passed, is the "Penn Station" of interiors. Its auditorium, redesigned by Carrère & Hastings in 1903, was not yet eligible for landmark protection. At the same time the still-young LPC was fending off plans that would have gutted Grand Central Terminal. The Metropolitan Museum of Art planned to remove its grand interior staircase. The public rooms of the Plaza Hotel had recently been redecorated. But the landmarks law offered no recourse to such losses until it was significantly amended in 1973 under Mayor John Lindsay, extending the designation process to public interiors, and city-owned scenic landmarks as well.

If the old Met was the "Penn Station" of interiors, then Radio City Music Hall was the "Grand Central." The first interior designations after 1973 were parts of the New York Public Library, historic house museums, City Hall—incontrovertibly "public" spaces. The Tax Reform Act of 1976 gave tax incentives for the preservation of historic properties used to produce income, encouraging building owners to rehabilitate older buildings and support their protection as landmarks. By 1978, LPC was considering the designation of the Chrysler Building lobby, the Town Hall performance space, and Radio City—privately owned, commercial spaces. Yet, despite owner opposition and some internal doubts about whether it could defend such direct involvement— interference, even—with the use of a space, LPC designated Radio City's extensive interior, from the grand foyer to the auditorium to the lounges. Almost simultaneously, in 1978, the United States Supreme Court handed down its milestone decision upholding the LPC's authority to regulate the construction of a tower on top of Grand Central Terminal. It was a galvanizing moment, for if the landmarks law could not save Grand Central or Radio City, what could it save?

Another major challenge presented itself in 1982, when the Helen Hayes, Morosco, and three other Broadway theaters were demolished to make way for the Marriott Marquis hotel in Times Square. As protestors swarmed the site, the LPC launched a survey of midtown theaters and began holding public hearings to weigh their potential for landmark designation, both inside and out. The theater owners mounted a counter-campaign, arguing that landmark protection would be "fatal" to Broadway. The reality has been anything but. For the two dozen theater interiors that were ultimately designated, LPC adopted guidelines that stressed preservation of the "overall form, shape and layout of auditoriums" while allowing ornamental detail to be removed for theatrical productions on the condition that it be restored post-production. Theater restoration, like that of the Belasco, has become mainstream.

The theater guidelines were a direct response to a specific political problem: owner opposition. But in the case of the former Manufacturers Trust Company building, its interior designated in 2011 and then immediately adapted from bank to retail use, LPC secured owner consent of interior designation by allowing fundamental changes to significant design features including the reconfiguration of the bank's prominent escalators (the modern equivalent of a grand Beaux-Arts staircase). This time, in the attempt to save the original interior design, it was preservationists who challenged the commission's use of its authority under the Landmarks Law.

As the Manufacturers Trust case suggests, the Landmarks Law gives LPC broad discretion to decide not only what to designate (the exterior of the building was designated in 1997, nearly fifteen years before its equally significant interior) but also how to regulate it.

There are four basic approaches to historic preservation. The first is conservation, which is maintaining the property exactly as it is, arresting deterioration but avoiding changes or replacements of any elements, as is done with ancient ruins, or well-maintained sites like the Film Center Building lobby. The second is restoration, which involves replacing and repairing missing parts or removing later additions so that the property appears as it did at a particular moment in time but only in a way that ensures that the changes can be reversed, as was done in the Empire State Building and the Merchant's House Museum The third approach is reconstruction and involves re-creating decorative elements from archival research, or fragments of the originals, to make exact facsimiles, as was done in the restoration of Radio City Music Hall and the Belasco Theater.

The fourth approach, adaptive reuse, can sometimes involve extensive changes to physical fabric. Over a period of time, historic buildings and interiors may outlive their original uses; changing customs, business mergers, technological development, and the fluctuations of fashion have made them unsuited to the purpose for which they were designed. In the past, such spaces might have been demolished, but growing public support of preservation has led to an interest in adaptive reuse, and recent years have seen the transformation of, for example, the Williamsburgh and Bowery Savings Banks into retail stores and event spaces, of lobbies like that of the Woolworth Building and the RKO Keith's theater into condominium entrances, theaters such as the Mark Hellinger and Loew's Paradise into places of worship, and other once-anachronistic adaptations that have preserved historic interiors and given them productive new lives.

An owner chooses which approach, or combination of approaches, to pursue, balancing aesthetic values with functional and economic ones. In the case of interior landmarks, the landmarks law gives LPC the final word on what work is appropriate based simply on whether it would "change, destroy or affect" any architectural feature—again, with broad discretion. "Use" is explicitly beyond LPC's purview. The theater guidelines and, more recently, bank guidelines, which distinguish between significant and non-significant design features and set up a process for removing teller counters and allowing for other "state of the art banking changes," represent LPC's efforts to sidestep use conflicts. Even when adaptive reuse, not to mention intensified security concerns post-9/11 (the Woolworth Building lobby, for example), has limited the public accessibility of an interior contrary to the intent of the law, LPC has avoided interference.

A persistent blind spot for preservation is design of the recent past. Penn Station, Grand Central, Radio City, the Chrysler Building were all between forty and fifty years old when they became threatened. Today, the youngest landmark interior, the Ford Foundation Building, dates to 1967, although designs up to 1985 now qualify. Will the most recent eligible interiors survive long enough to be considered for landmark protection?

Part of the reason for this lag is changing taste. It often takes the distance of at least a generation to appreciate the enduring value of design. But modern interiors are especially sensitive. Where facades are transparent, interiors and exteriors are inextricably connected. In minimalist spaces, identifying decorative elements are often in the furnishings rather than in plasterwork or ceiling ornament. Seagram Building owners balked at LPC's 1989 designation of the Four Seasons restaurant interior, arguing that without its furnishings it would be "a void, without any particular architectural character." Time will tell whether landmark designation that excludes furnishings is adequate to protect the design integrity of such interiors.

This book tells the stories of forty-seven interior landmarks, from the oldest to the youngest, their histories and designers, the challenges of saving them, the restorations or re-imaginings that preserved them or gave them new life, and the communities, preservationists, philanthropists, politicians, designers and artisans who made it all possible. They are from every borough, encompassing a variety of styles, and many different functions. Some were unanimously accepted as worthy of designation, others were hotly contested, sometimes in contentious legal battles. Some were proposed by building owners, some by grassroots neighborhood groups, some by business alliances, some by design enthusiasts, some by preservationists. Their beauty, as with all things, may be in the eye of the beholder, but their merit as documents of specific times and place is indisputable.

City Hall

1811

City Hall Park, Manhattan
John McComb Jr. and Joseph-François Mangin
Interior designated 1976

This graceful building in a small park in Lower Manhattan is a piece of New York history and a cosmopolitan mix of styles evoking the diversity of the city itself. Reflecting the collaboration between an American, John McComb Jr., and a French emigré, Joseph-François Mangin, its Federal architecture is embellished with Gallic touches that acknowledge the new republic's debt to its Revolutionary War ally. America's oldest continuous seat of municipal government and the city's oldest interior landmark, City Hall was among the first to be designated after the landmarks law was amended to allow protection of interiors in 1973.

The building is actually New York City's third City Hall: the first was built in the seventeenth century on Pearl Street, and another predecessor was on the site of what is now Federal Hall. The design was selected in a competition (Benjamin Latrobe, architect of the U.S.

Capitol, was among the twenty-six entrants) that brought a prize of $350 and considerable prestige to the winners. Dedicated on July 4, 1811, to mark Independence Day, the building was occupied the following year.

Tall, arched doorways at the portico open into an elegant white-marble entrance hall that leads to a double-height central rotunda. Its grand coffered dome is supported by ten fluted Corinthian columns and culminates in an oculus that floods the interior with natural light. The cantilevered, curved double staircase, decorated with floral and vine motifs, leads to the monumental second floor, where classical ornament on walls and doorways adds to the stateliness of the space.

The pristine beauty of the interiors today belies their crisis-ridden history. In addition to surviving two fires, City Hall prevailed against repeated threats to its existence, including late nineteenth-century City Beautiful redevelopment plans to replace it with a new executive office building. Even the *New York Times* favored demolition or relocation to one of several proposed sites, including either Bryant or Central Park. Echoing widespread public protest, *Harper's* magazine editorialized that its destruction would be regarded "not

The balcony was added in 1858, and the painted iron balustrade, based on McComb's original drawings, was part of the interior restoration begun by Grosvenor Atterbury in 1907.

From the bottom of the stairs, the interior is almost an abstract composition of concentric forms. In the latest restoration, the ceiling rosettes on the dome were individually secured by plaster-covered steel bolts.

only as a municipal calamity, but as an act of vandalism." The threat subsided in 1894, when New York State passed a law prohibiting demolition of the historic building, and in 1907, architect Grosvenor Atterbury oversaw the first comprehensive restoration of the interior, reviving its original grandeur.

Although City Hall escaped destruction or relocation, it was not adequately maintained. Shreve, Lamb and Harmon had overseen some restoration in 1956, but little more was attempted for more than half a century. By the 1970s, the need to preserve City Hall was clear. The designation of its interiors in 1976, along with Federal Hall and the Surrogate's Court, reflected the Landmarks Preservation Commission's concern with protecting the city's most historic and symbolic structures, both inside and out.

But it was not until 1997, when a large plaster rosette fell from the dome into the rotunda, that an extensive renovation was undertaken under the direction of Beyer Blinder Belle Architects & Planners. The project repaired water damage to the interiors and removed elements from interim repairs that required reconstructing moldings, replacing ceiling ornamentation, and stabilizing the staircase. Equally important, the infrastructure was updated to bring the masonry and wood building in line with modern safety codes.

The interior of City Hall is now as beautiful as when it was completed more than two centuries ago. It is both a symbol of civic pride for the nation's greatest city and a fine example of the sensitive preservation of a historic building.

Old Merchant's House

1832

In the twin first-floor parlors, the decorative surround is Greek Revival, but the bronze-and-cut-glass chandeliers and some of the mahogany furniture are in the later Renaissance Revival style.

29 East Fourth Street, Manhattan
Joseph Brewster, builder
Interior designated 1981

A time capsule of early nineteenth-century residential life in a twenty-first-century metropolis, the Old Merchant's House (also known as the Seabury Tredwell House and now the Merchant's House Museum) retains not only its original architecture but also its interiors and furnishings. It was among the earliest buildings designated by the Landmarks Preservation Commission, which called it a "unique document of its period."

Seabury Tredwell was a prosperous merchant who purchased the three-year-old townhouse for the considerable sum of $18,000. Located near Astor Place in what was becoming the most fashionable part of the city, the substantial redbrick building has a Federal-style exterior, although the fluted Doric columns flanking the entrance offer a foretaste of the interiors, which are decorated in the latest fashion, Greek Revival.

Typical for row houses of its time, the Seabury Tredwell house has three-and-a-half floors, with a kitchen and family dining/living areas in the English basement. The first floor contains a pair of formal parlors, bedrooms are on the second and third, and servants' quarters (not included in the interior landmark designation) are on the half-floor above. The arched entry opens into a vestibule, where faux-marble walls and egg-and-dart molding introduce the neoclassical scheme. The vestibule leads to the first of the identical parlors separated by mahogany pocket doors. Each has tall windows extending almost from floor to ceiling, black marble fireplaces, and a red-on-gold wall-to-wall carpet patterned after the mosaic tile floors excavated at Pompeii and Herculaneum. Bronze and cut-glass chandeliers are suspended from ornate ceiling rosettes. Other architectural features include corner pilasters, wraparound entablatures, egg-and-dart and foliate moldings, and acanthus and anthemion motifs. When the pocket doors are opened, the white-walled rooms (typical for the time) form one large space for entertaining. The rear parlor later became the dining room.

On the second floor, accessed by an elegant staircase with mahogany and brass railings, are two identical bedrooms directly over the parlors. They are ornamented with similar but less elaborate plasterwork and gray-veined white marble fireplaces. Geometric-patterned carpet covers the front bedroom floor. A narrow hall bedroom, intended for a child, connects to the front master bedroom.

The multipurpose family area in the basement level is warm toned, with peach walls and a black-and-gold marble fireplace. A spacious kitchen was outfitted with a cast-iron stove for both heating and cooking, a brick oven and warming cupboard, and a stone sink with a copper hand pump.

Members of the Tredwell family occupied the house continuously until Seabury's last surviving daughter,

a recluse, died in 1933 at the age of ninety-three. Some redecorating had taken place over the years, keeping up with the current fashions to enhance the Tredwell daughters' matrimonial prospects, but the interiors were essentially intact.

As the house was about to be put up for sale, George Chapman, a distant cousin, saved it from foreclosure and established a nonprofit society to operate it as a museum. In 1936, after some renovation, including the conversion

---

In the kitchen on the lower level, the cast-iron stove is recessed into the brick-walled fireplace. The painted wood door conceals the dumbwaiter, which brought food up to the dining room.

of the gas chandeliers to electricity, it opened as the Merchant's House Museum. Following Chapman's death, however, its condition declined. In 1962 the civic-minded and well-connected Decorators Club, the country's oldest organization of professional designers, stepped in to raise funds for its restoration. Three years later, the house was declared one of the city's first landmarks under the new law, but despite these efforts, the museum closed in 1970.

It was brought back with the help of city, state, and private funds. Beginning in 1968, the architect Joseph Roberto directed a nine-year restoration that included structural work, repainting, restoring ornamental plaster-work, reinstalling the original furniture, reproducing curtains, and reweaving carpets. The museum reopened in November 1979.

Since 1990, Jan Hird Pokorny Associates has over-seen its maintenance and restoration, and a long-term Historic Furnishings Plan, initiated in 2007, has involved in-depth analysis of paint finishes and research into original fabrics, as well as archival research into Tredwell family history. The years 1835 to 1865 were identified as the period of significance for the restoration of the interiors. The family dining/living area was repainted in warmer colors, the ground floor hall carpet was removed to reveal original pine board floors, and additional work is progressing. Since 1999 the house has been managed by the Historic House Trust in association with the Department of Parks and Recreation.

The mannequin displays one of the Tredwell family's silk gowns. In the far corner of the bedroom is a curtained child's bed.

The parlor chandeliers, originally gas but converted to electricity in the late nineteenth century, are suspended from elaborate plaster rosettes.

Bartow-Pell Mansion

1842

In the elegantly appointed parlors, mahogany furniture and window treatment reflect the fashionable Greek Revival style, in contrast to the Federal exterior of the building.

895 Shore Road, Bronx
Minard Lafever, Delano & Aldrich
Interior designated 1975

The Bartow-Pell Mansion is the only survivor of the grand nineteenth-century estates built on the shores of Long Island Sound, a lush suburban setting within the city itself.

The bucolic site was once part of a 50,000-acre tract of land comprising much of what became the Bronx and lower Westchester County. It was purchased by Thomas Pell in 1654 from the Siwanoy Indians. Reduced to a modest 220 acres after the Revolutionary War, the estate was acquired by Pell's descendant Robert Bartow, who commissioned the present Federal-style gray stone mansion; the design is attributed to Minard Lafever.

The spacious entrance hall is dominated by an elegant staircase that spirals upward to the string of clerestory windows rimming the rooftop. The hall opens onto the formal dining room and the parlor beyond, identical spaces separated by mahogany pocket doors.

In both rooms, mahogany furniture is complemented by soft green walls, white moldings, light-colored marble fireplaces, and a multicolored carpet with a pattern of classical motifs. French windows in the parlor open to the garden and views of Long Island Sound. Greek Revival architectural details abound: pilasters frame pedimented doorways, pocket doors, and windows; carved anthemia and acanthus leaves ornament the woodwork; and chandeliers hang from plaster ceiling rosettes.

The Bartow family occupied the house from 1842 to 1888, when Mrs. Bartow gave it to the city. Vacant from 1888 to 1914, the house and its interiors deteriorated until the International Garden Club leased the property from the city in exchange for a promise to restore and manage it. The civic-minded group retained Delano & Aldrich to restore the interiors to the Greek Revival style in which they were originally decorated and also to restore the much-admired formal gardens.

The project was noteworthy as an early example of privately funded restoration, predating the Rockefellers' program for Colonial Williamsburg and well before proposals for landmarks legislation gained traction. Elsewhere in the United States, "period rooms" were

The freestanding cantilever staircase spirals from ground floor to attic, framed in graceful turned-wood balusters, and lit by small clerestory windows at roof level.

The underside of the staircase creates the effect of a lowered ceiling in the entry.

An exuberantly sculptural Empire sofa in the parlor.

The marble mantelpieces in the twin parlors are carved with graceful classical ornament.

often removed from their original contexts and installed in museums such as the Metropolitan Museum of Art and Philadelphia Museum of Art. At Bartow-Pell, the preserved interiors remained in situ, serving as headquarters for the International Garden Club, which opened the house to the public as a museum in 1946. Before becoming a museum, the mansion played host to some of New York's most prominent citizens, including Mayor Fiorello La Guardia, who used it as his summer residence in 1936. Today the property is owned by the city and managed by the Historic House Trust in association with the New York City Department of Parks and Recreation.

Sailors Snug Harbor

Building "C" 1833, Chapel 1856

The painted ornament on the elliptical dome of Building "C" includes foliate panels, scalloped pilasters, and an iron fence. The skylight is centered with a compass and an eight-pointed star, echoed by one on the floor directly beneath.

1000 Richmond Terrace, Staten Island
Minard Lafever, James Solomon
Charles Berry, interior designer
Interiors designated 1982

This bucolic complex originated as a home for "aged, decrepit and worn-out sailors"—one of America's first charitable institutions. It was established through the philanthropy of Robert Richard Randall, a merchant and seafarer who bequeathed his twenty-four-acre Manhattan estate near Washington Square in Greenwich Village, then a rural area, for the retirement home. When land values in the neighborhood skyrocketed, the trustees received approval to modify Randall's will and build the institution in another location, and in 1831 they purchased a 130-acre site on Staten Island overlooking New York Bay. Even though many of the original buildings at Sailors Snug Harbor have been demolished, the complex is one of the most important examples of Greek Revival architecture in the country.

Sailors Snug Harbor opened in 1833 with thirty-seven residents, but by the turn of the century it had about a thousand occupants, dubbed Snugs. The sole requirement for residence was five years of service in the U.S. Navy. Income from rents on the original land (now Washington Mews) supported the association, which at its largest included fifty-five buildings: dormitories, staff residences, a hospital, a chapel, and also a cemetery, which remains on the grounds today.

Although it was a charity, the trustees wanted the project to have architectural merit, and as was customary at the time, a design competition was held for the central structure—now called Building "C"—which would define the character of the complex. It is the first known project of the winner, Minard Lafever, who designed a striking marble building with a grand Ionic portico and a spare but dramatic interior. In 1884 Charles Berry added the exuberant and colorful ornamentation.

The two-and-a-half-story rectangular space features a groined-arch ceiling crowned by an elliptical dome. A wraparound gallery leads to private rooms,

and transverse halls provide access to the adjacent buildings. Barry's decor combines Neo-Grec style with fanciful late nineteenth-century eclecticism. Classical elements such as dark cherry wood pilasters, carved lintels framing the doors, and a Greek fret border on the ash floor coexist with colorful nautical-themed motifs on the walls, frescoed ceiling, and stained-glass windows.

The other interior landmark in Snug Harbor is the chapel, designed by builder-architect James Solomon in the Italianate style. It was originally a modest rectangular space with arched windows, a raised altar platform, simple wood pews, and carved wainscoting. In 1873 Berry embellished the interior with trompe l'oeil architectural details. Multipaned stained-glass windows were added a decade later.

Despite its historic significance, Sailors Snug Harbor was almost destroyed; by the 1960s, dozens

Beneath painted ornament and carved wood trim, founder Robert Richard Randall is memorialized on a wall of the main hall.

of its buildings were gone. The Landmarks Preservation Commission used its new authority under the 1965 landmarks law to designate six of the remaining structures as individual landmarks, defying a threat by Snug Harbor trustees to "lock the doors and let the buildings rot." The trustees sued, an early test of the constitutional authority of the commission. The designation was upheld by the Appellate Division of the New York State Supreme Court, affirming the city's right to restrict an owner's use of property "for the cultural and aesthetic benefit of the Community" and establishing important criteria for determining the impact of landmark designation on nonprofit institutions.

Landmark designation alone, however, could not save Sailors Snug Harbor. In 1971, to avoid further legal challenges by trustees of the financially strapped institution, Mayor John V. Lindsay organized the city's purchase of the designated buildings, one as a new home for the Staten Island Museum, and the surrounding 13.3 acres; the trustees sold an additional 65 acres to the city and relocated the institution to North Carolina. In 1976 the city began to transform the complex into the Snug Harbor Cultural Center. The buildings and grounds now house not only the Staten Island Museum but also a maritime museum, a children's museum, an art gallery, a concert hall, artist studios, a botanical garden, and a Chinese scholar's garden.

This frescoed corner of the groin-vaulted ceiling of the main hall foliage incorporates both foliage and sea serpents.

The chapel ornament is simple, with trompe l'oeil architectural details. Stained-glass windows were a later addition.

Federal Hall
National Memorial

1842

The masonry saucer dome, set beneath the roof but still supporting considerable weight, was an engineering achievement in its time.

---

26 Wall Street, Manhattan
Town & Davis, Samuel Thomson, John Frazee
Interior designated 1975

Anchoring the intersection of Wall and Nassau Streets in what is now the financial district of Manhattan, the imposing white Tuckahoe marble structure now known as Federal Hall has served as both a temple to finance and a patriotic symbol. Originally the New York Custom House, Federal Hall is now a museum honoring George Washington, whose statue stands on a pedestal on the building's front steps.

The original building on the site, completed in 1700, was New York's second City Hall. In 1788 it was remodeled and enlarged by Pierre L'Enfant and was renamed Federal Hall a year later, when it became the nation's first Capitol under the Constitution. It was there that the first Congress met, the Bill of Rights was written, and the first president was inaugurated in 1789. The capital moved to Philadelphia in 1790, and the structure was demolished in 1812.

When Ithiel Town and Alexander Jackson Davis won the competition to design the Custom House in 1833, Town & Davis was the leading architectural firm in New York, and one of the country's first professional architectural offices, founded in 1829. Though they worked in several revival styles (Alexander Jackson Davis completed Gothic Revival Lyndhurst the same year as Federal Hall), the partners were strong proponents of Greek Revival, which would become the style of choice for civic architecture as well as financial, arts, and educational institutions. The original Town & Davis plans were modified, first by Samuel Thomson, superintendent of construction for the government, and then by his successor, sculptor John Frazee, who is thought to be responsible for most of the rich interior detail.

The great rotunda is bordered by sixteen fluted Corinthian columns, each cut from a single block of marble, beneath a simple entablature that anchors a broad, low dome with a central skylight projecting above the roofline but not visible from the street. In place of coffering, the dome has tapered plasterwork panels with anthemion motifs; a series of rosettes adorn the ring

Fluted Corinthian columns and pilasters with intricately carved capitals define the 1,500-square-foot rotunda.

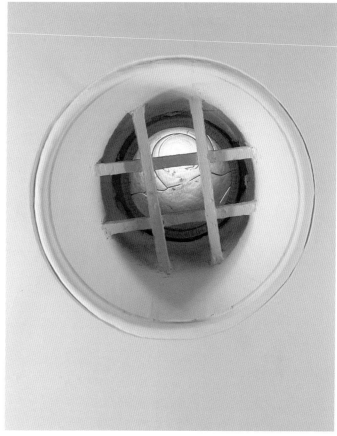

During the tenure of the U.S. Treasury, gold and silver bouillon was stored behind these mixed-metal doors.

Glass inserts in the rotunda floor admit light to the basement level. The view from below extends to the skylight.

beneath the skylight. Around the perimeter is a balcony with gilded ironwork railings incorporating caryatids and foliate motifs. The marble floor is inlaid with concentric rings in tones of gray; at its center is the stone slab on which Washington stood to take his oath of office.

The imposing architecture of the building reflects the importance of the Customs Service, which had responsibility for collecting revenues from imports and exports in the nation's major commercial center. In 1862, when customs operations moved to larger quarters, the building became the New York branch of the U.S. Sub-Treasury, housing gold and silver reserves in basement vaults. The formation of the Federal Reserve in 1920 made this function obsolete, and a passport office and other agencies occupied the building until 1955, when it became a museum devoted to the history of New York City, administered by the National Park Service.

It is now a memorial to the first president and the democratic ideals that inspired America's founders.

The events of September 11, 2001, shook Federal Hall to its core—literally. Already compromised by time and deferred maintenance, cracks, cosmetic deterioration, and weaknesses in the foundation were exacerbated by the collapse of the nearby World Trade Center towers. The Park Service closed the building in 2004 to undertake repairs, orchestrated by Einhorn Yaffee Prescott Architecture & Engineering. The structure was stabilized, interior plaster refaced, the original cream paint color restored, and partitions on the office floors removed to reveal the original architectural details.

Federal Hall reopened to the public in 2006 as a museum and educational center; an appropriate setting for exhibitions related the nation's history. Its basement now houses a branch of the National Archives, the first outside of Washington, D.C.

Tweed Courthouse

1881

Roy Lichtenstein's sculpture *Element E* was installed in the lobby in 2003 as part of the exhibition "Roy Lichtenstein at City Hall," organized by the Public Art Fund.

52 Chambers Street, Manhattan
John Kellum, Leopold Eidlitz
Interior designated 1984

The second-oldest extant government building in the city (built seventy years after City Hall), the infamous Tweed Courthouse (officially, the New York County Courthouse) has been a touchstone for controversy since construction began in 1861. It contains what the Landmarks Preservation Commission called "one of the few and one of the best remaining grand Italianate interior spaces in the city," and the story behind the space is equally noteworthy.

Built in City Hall Park on a site that was once occupied by an almshouse, the building was the centerpiece of the largest corruption case in New York history. Tammany Hall boss William M. Tweed used the project to embezzle city funds, and the discovery of frauds linked to the construction halted work before the building was completed. "Boss" Tweed was convicted and jailed, but the scandal irrevocably tainted the courthouse image.

John Kellum, the original architect, had designed the celebrated A. T. Stewart department store on Broadway and 10th Street (destroyed by fire in 1956), as well as the original New York Stock Exchange. Thomas Little, a political appointee, worked with him on the building. Kellum died in 1871 after completing just two floors of the rotunda, and in 1876 Leopold Eidlitz was retained to complete the project. A skilled architect and theorist who shared John Ruskin's preference for medieval styles, he interjected his personal aesthetic—his Assembly Chamber in Albany's State Capitol prefigures elements of the Tweed interiors, which are a composite of Kellum's and Eidlitz's contrasting styles.

The courthouse was intended as a monumental civic structure in the tradition of the United States Capitol—a dome was designed but never built. Kellum was a pioneer in the structural use of cast iron in architecture, and used it extensively in the courthouse. By the mid-nineteenth century, cast iron had become a widely used and often highly decorative alternative to masonry; it was inexpensive, strong, and fireproof. Though there are many buildings with cast-iron facades, the Tweed courthouse is the only known surviving cast-iron interior in the city.

Within the five-level interior (on the exterior it appears to have only three and a half stories), thirty courtrooms are arranged around a central core, an octagonal, eighty-five-foot-high rotunda—a light-filled, airy open space with two symmetrical wings, elaborate cast-iron staircases on either side, and an octagonal skylight. Around the perimeter, the walls and broad, Romanesque-style arches on squat columns with foliate capitals are faced in cream, black, and red brickwork with diamond insets and crenellation. On the second floor, originally the main level, the medieval ambience competes with Kellum's classical pedimented niches, columns and pilasters, and cast-iron railings. Eidlitz was criticized for designing in a style that conflicted with the exterior and was considered inappropriate for a civic building.

Throughout its history, the courthouse's image was undermined by its mismatched decor as well as its association with Tweed. The interior suffered several unfortunate renovations: in 1908 the rotunda was painted gray to cover the multicolored brickwork and the columns were marbleized; in later years doors were changed, areas repainted, and the stained-glass skylight removed, but the rotunda remained intact.

In 1927 the County Court moved to new quarters, and the building became a city courthouse. From 1961 on it held municipal offices—an awkward transition for the large courtrooms. Like City Hall, the Tweed Courthouse was threatened by plans to redevelop the civic center. Disrespected and perceived as obsolete, the building had been proposed for demolition as early as the 1890s, but the threat grew serious in 1974, when the city administration proposed razing it to build a new executive office building.

Preservationists and key political figures (including council member Robert F. Wagner Jr. and mayoral candidate Edward I. Koch) formed an emergency Save the Tweed Committee, arguing against derision of the "notorious" structure and relying on growing public interest in preservation and "recycling." The 1970s fiscal crisis ended the debate and saved the building, which was found to be less costly to renovate than to replace. In 1975 the private nonprofit New York Landmarks Conservancy stepped in to oversee critical repairs, using Federal public-works grants. By the time the Landmarks Preservation Commission held hearings on the Tweed Courthouse, there were no opponents to designation, acknowledging the building's historic importance as well as the uniqueness of its design.

In 1999 John G. Waite Associates began a major restoration, replacing skylights and marble and glass-tiled floors, repainting interiors in the original colors (including faux brick and gilding), and rebuilding the steep entrance steps that had been removed to widen Chambers Street. The project was completed in 2001, and the Tweed now houses the New York City Department of Education and a public school.

Along one of the two balconies, the contrast of styles: Kellum created large rectangular openings that Eidlitz filled in with arches in tricolor brickwork, supported by columns with foliate capitals.

Linear patterning on the ceiling complements the medieval-inspired brickwork arches.

Williamsburgh Savings Bank

1875

The absence of interior columns contributes to the monumental feeling of the space. Light from windows overhead highlights the detailing on pillars, painted frieze, and carved stone dado.

175 Broadway, Brooklyn
George B. Post
Interior designated 1996

Inside a distinguished classical building, the original headquarters of the Williamsburgh Savings Bank is a monumental space, one of the few such interiors surviving from the post–Civil War period, and one of the earliest examples of a new approach to the design of banks. Almost a century and a half later, refurbished and repurposed, it once more dazzles with rich color and intricate detailing that recall both pure classicism and its more extravagant Gilded Age flourishes.

At the time of the bank's founding, the classical vocabulary was the chosen expression for government buildings and major institutions like museums. Connoting dignity, stability, and trustworthiness, it was adopted as an equally appropriate idiom for banks. The 28,500-square-foot Williamsburgh Savings Bank was a precursor of the grand banking halls that came into fashion after the 1893 World's Columbian Exhibition in Chicago.

The architect, George B. Post, had worked with celebrated Beaux-Arts architect Richard Morris Hunt, and was also trained as an engineer. This expertise made him a good choice for the structurally complex building; engineering skill was also a factor in his work on the Long Island Historical Society and the Metropolitan Museum of Art. The architect's later buildings also included the New York Stock Exchange and the principal buildings of the City College campus.

A pedimented portico and bronze doors lead into the great banking hall dominated by a cast-iron dome that transitions, via pendentives and broad arches, to an unobstructed, column-free square. Light floods into the space through twenty oval windows encircling the dome, and large windows on three perimeter walls. The interior of the dome is embellished with a brilliantly colored, intricate pattern of geometric and floral motifs by Peter B. Wight, an influential architect and painter whose Venetian-Gothic-inspired designs reflected the influence of theorist John Ruskin. The classical vocabulary of the space itself—massive arches framed in clusters of granite, marble-topped columns, carved stone dado, and rows of gilded rosettes—contrasts with ornament in a more

The original dome, with Peter B. Wight's painted ornament, contrasts with the more conventionally classic form of the dome for the women's banking hall.

The original teller windows are now filled with mirrored glass.

The original "birdcage" elevator.

eclectic vein. A painted frieze, bands of foliate carving, and a marble mosaic floor complete a space that is at once monumental and inviting, in an unusual synthesis of styles.

In 1908 another domed section was added to create a separate banking hall for women depositors, an increasing proportion of the bank's clientele as women, now permitted to own property, began to achieve financial independence. Less elaborate than the first, the coffered dome has a leaded-glass oculus. Throughout both halls, ornamental details underscore the bank's position as one of the city's leading and most prosperous institutions of its kind. In the last half of the twentieth century, however, it fell victim to competition, consolidations, and the waning need for specialized local banks. At the time of landmark designation, the elaborate marble floor was covered with carpet, the surviving panels of the secondary dome's skylight had been put into storage, and the archway between the two banking rooms was blocked by drywall.

HSBC Bank took over the Williamsburgh Savings Bank in a 1996 merger and moved to another location, selling the building in 2010. The interior continued to languish, its beauty buried beneath layers of dirt, trash,

and drywall, the dome painting flaking off, the marble flooring cracked and chipped.

Taking advantage of federal tax credits that had been introduced in 1986 to encourage rehabilitation and adaptive reuse of historic buildings, the new owners undertook a three-year rescue and rehabilitation project that involved not only restoring the ornamentation of the domes and repairing or replicating bronze hardware but also installing miles of heating tubes beneath a new marble floor (a faithful replica of the original) and air-conditioning units. Other rescued and restored treasures include the 1875 French vault door and the 1911 birdcage elevator, one of only three in the city still operating in its original state.

The Williamsburgh Savings Bank emerged in 2014 with a new identity as an event venue, in a restoration overseen by David Scott Parker Architects. It was wittily renamed Weylin B. Seymour's to justify retaining the ubiquitous WSB monograms (some old, others newly added) on windows, staircases, doorknobs, and even hinges. Though far from what its original designer envisioned, the banking hall now astonishes visitors as it once did depositors.

Seventh Regiment Armory

1881

643 Park Avenue, Manhattan
Charles W. Clinton, Robinson & Knust
Interior designated 1994

Housing the largest group of Aesthetic Movement interiors in America, the Seventh Regiment Armory (now known as the Park Avenue Armory) was described by the Landmarks Preservation Commission as "the height of American interior design within a single building for a single client." That client was the New York State National Guard, and the rooms reflect the taste and prestige of the companies of the "Silk Stocking Regiment."

Armories, built to house the country's volunteer state militias and provide space for training and equipment storage, were generally fortresslike, government-funded brick structures with functional interiors, but they also served as social centers for their members. The armory on Park Avenue was one of the most elaborate of the genre, and the only armory to be privately financed, with funds raised by the regiment that would occupy it.

Clinton, an architect and veteran of the regiment,

was awarded the commission to design the building. The plan followed that of nineteenth-century railroad stations, with a "headhouse" facing Park Avenue and a drill shed to the rear. In addition to the drill hall, offices, and storage space, there are eighteen rooms furnished by the country's most prominent decorators and cabinetmakers, including Herter Brothers, Louis Comfort Tiffany & Co., Associated Artists, Alexander Roux, Pottier & Stymus, Sidney V. Stratton, and Kimbel & Cabus. Decorating had recently emerged as a profession distinct from architecture, and it was customary for affluent clients to hire these specialists to decorate their homes and private clubs. But, because few Gilded Age townhouses and mansions remain intact—and, in any case, private interiors do not qualify for landmark designation—the armory's rooms are among the very few still in existence and available for public view.

Massive oak doors open onto the wainscoted foyer, which leads up a few steps to the entrance hall and main corridor, and from there to the Drill Hall—one of the largest unobstructed spaces in the city, and the oldest extant balloon shed. Its barrel-vaulted ceiling is supported by broad wrought-iron trusses, a structural

system previously used only in railroad stations. Engineer Charles Macdonald, a bridge specialist, and architect Robert G. Hatfield consulted on the complex design. Seating along all four sides accommodated almost 1,100, and gaslights were suspended from the roof.

The most formal rooms in the building are on the main level of the headhouse. The celebrated Veterans Room and the adjacent Library are among the few extant interiors by Louis Comfort Tiffany and the Associated Artists decorating firm. The fireplace in the Veterans Room features vivid turquoise and blue glass tile, with a carved-wood mantel supported by slender colonettes. The coffered-wood ceiling is intricately stenciled, complementing the metalwork of the light fixtures. The Library has a barrel-vaulted ceiling covered in cast-plaster panels in a basketweave pattern, with two tiers of mahogany bookcases and a gallery wrapping the walls.

The prestigious firm of Herter Brothers designed five rooms in the armory, including three on the main floor: the Reception Room, which has stenciled walls, a coved ceiling, and woodwork by Alexander Roux; the Board of Officers Room, featuring dark mahogany woodwork and stenciled ornament; and the Colonel's Room, paneled in French black walnut, with a central mantel, built-in cabinetry, and furniture by Marcotte & Company. Pottier & Stymus designed the Field & Staff Room. On the second floor, individual companies, A to K, each commissioned its own clubroom; this group, each in a different style, includes interiors by Herter Brothers, Pottier & Stymus, and others.

Though the armory's exceptional interiors were favorably received by the public and the regiment alike, the building underwent considerable change, including installation of electricity and steam heat and the construction of two additional floors. Some of the many modifications responded to new uses and changing tastes. The Drill Hall was altered in 1913 to increase seating capacity to three thousand; windows were bricked over, the floor was refinished, and lighting fixtures were replaced. In 1900 the library collections were removed from the shelves, and the room served as an office before

becoming a regimental museum. Many of the first- and second-floor rooms were repainted or redecorated, but the Veterans Room remained essentially intact, although in the ceiling was overpainted and the walls were stripped of the original Tiffany wallpaper and hung with velvet.

New York's National Guard continued to use the armory, but most of the rooms were badly neglected for many years. Despite designation of the armory's exterior in 1967 and the interior in 1994, the damage was becoming critical. In 2000, the World Monuments Fund named the Seventh Regiment Armory one of the world's "100 Most Endangered Historic Sites."

In 2007, the newly formed Seventh Regiment Armory Conservancy was given a ninety-nine-year lease on the building from New York State, with a mandate to transform it into a cultural institution that supports "unconventional works in the performing and visual arts that need non-traditional spaces for their full realization."

The group commissioned Herzog & de Meuron, in conjunction with Platt Byard Dovell White Architects, to renovate, restore, and repair the historic fabric and to install modern MEP and code-compliant systems.

The architects' approach is described as "delayering," a process of studying the evolution of each space to determine which original elements to restore, which alterations to preserve, and which to remove to reveal

The Veterans Room, the most famous of the Armory interiors, was a collaboration of the Associated Artists, led by Louis Comfort Tiffany, Samuel Colman, and Candace Wheeler, and Stanford White.

Slender colonettes, with intricately carved capitals support the mantel. Brilliant blue tiles by Tiffany surround the fireplace.

historical layers, an innovative interpretive strategy for restoration of a landmark that has been approved by the State Historic Preservation Office as well as LPC.

The project has proceded in stages. The Board of Officers Room has become an intimate performance space, and the Drill Hall is a venue for avant-garde art installations, dance, and theater in a space unlike any other in the city. Restoration of the Veterans Room will be completed in December 2015.

Long Island Historical Society Building

In the Othmer Library, intricately carved colonettes mark the end panels of bookcases set perpendicular to the walls.

1881

128 Pierrepont Street, Brooklyn
George B. Post
Interior designated 1982

One of the most architecturally significant landmarks in the Brooklyn Heights Historic District, this handsome Renaissance Revival building attests to the importance of local historical societies in the nineteenth century, when this type of cultural institution became popular. The building itself was advanced for its time: the exterior is distinguished by substantial use of ornamental terra-cotta—one of the first architectural uses of the material in the city—and the interiors combine industrial technology with traditional craftsmanship.

The society was founded by Henry Pierrepont as the Long Island Historical Society in 1863, when Brooklyn (then an independent city) was the cultural and commercial center of Long Island. In December 1877 a competition was announced for the design of its headquarters, and fourteen major architects submitted proposals. George B. Post, trained as an engineer as well as an architect, had designed commercial buildings—a significant qualification, as the specifications called for modern fireproofing and ventilation. Many of Post's important buildings are gone—among them the Equitable Life Assurance Building, an archetype for the skyscraper, and the World Building, for a time the city's tallest.

Warm-toned black ash is the primary material used throughout the interior. The entry features paneled wainscoting and a floor of geometrically patterned Minton tile. An L-shaped, richly detailed carved-wood staircase leads to the second floor, where double doors open onto the building's principal room, the Othmer Library. The space is both impressive and intimate, with a two-story atrium surrounded by a gallery that projects somewhat over the main level. The twenty-four supporting columns combine technology with craft: they are made of iron encased in machine- and hand-carved wood. Slimmer than if they had been solid wood, the swagged and fluted columns admit maximum natural light into the lower level from the round-headed windows on three sides. Geometrically patterned stained glass fills the window lunettes. The light-filled central space is a counterpoint to the rich colors and textures of

the rows of books in carved bookcases, set perpendicular to the walls. Graceful chandeliers and reading lamps of brass and frosted glass complete the decorative scheme.

Over the years, the library has acquired major collections, including genealogical, property, and municipal records; historical maps and atlases; and documents related to slavery and abolition. Unique attractions include the Brooklyn Dodgers' 1955 World Series Championship banner and a copy of the Emancipation Proclamation signed by Abraham Lincoln. In October 1985, in recognition of the focus of its programs and its support from the community, the organization changed its name to the Brooklyn Historical Society. It now owns the most comprehensive collection of Brooklyn-related materials (according to the organization, one in seven Americans can trace their family roots to Brooklyn).

In the 1980s, while the society was expanding its activities as a museum and education center, the building was becoming endangered. A leaking roof, malfunctioning elevator, and outdated heating system threatened the valuable library holdings. A bequest from benefactor and board member Donald Othmer in 1998 spearheaded fund-raising efforts and a major project by Jan Hird Pokorny Associates to restore the library and add educational space. Expected to take eighteen months, it took more than four years. Further renovations completed in the fall of 2013 added event and education facilities to serve the organization's expanding needs while preserving the original historic details. The 150-year-old Society continues to serve the borough whose history it documents, while its interiors are an attraction to visitors from any borough or any state.

Richly carved wood and a striking geometric-patterned ceramic tile floor enhance the entry and the stair hall. An unusual double-capital column supports the stair.

Gould Memorial Library

1899

Hall of Fame Terrace at Sedgwick Avenue, Bronx
McKim, Mead & White
Interior designated 1981

Unknown to many New Yorkers, this building is considered one of Stanford White's masterpieces. Built as the centerpiece of the Bronx campus of New York University, its Pantheon-inspired form has American antecedents in Thomas Jefferson's library at the University of Virginia (1826) and in countless civic and institutional buildings constructed after the 1893 World's Columbian Exposition in Chicago. The grand reading room, though now playing another role for a different institution, is as imposing today as it was when completed.

The University of the City of New York, founded in Washington Square in 1831, was renamed New York University in 1896. It was a relatively modest institution until Henry McCracken became chancellor in 1891. Aspiring to transform it into an "ideal American college," he believed that it could not attain that goal in a downtown commercial neighborhood and required a campus-like

setting area within easy reach of the city. A bequest from the daughter of the financier and railroad baron Jay Gould made it possible, and a site was chosen overlooking the Harlem River with a view of the Palisades.

McKim, Mead & White was chosen to design the facility over rival architects George B. Post, Henry Hardenburgh, and Richard Morris Hunt. While White was designing the New York University site, his partner Charles McKim was working on the main campus of rival Columbia University. The differences in the classical architecture of Gould Library and Columbia's Low Library reflect the individual architects' styles: McKim's aesthetic was more monumental and severe; White's, more inclined toward Beaux-Arts elegance and the importance of integrating buildings into their settings, typifying the tenets of the so-called American Renaissance era.

The Gould Memorial Library was the centerpiece of the campus, flanked by the Hall of Languages and the Hall of Philosophy—the three joined by an ambulatory, later to become the Hall of Fame colonnade, which houses bronze busts of prominent Americans. The brick library, approached through an allée of trees, is configured as a Greek cross. Its shallow wings transition to

The sixteen Connemara marble columns were shipped from Ireland in sections and assembled on site. The radiating sculptured bronze motif in the center of the floor was originally filled with glass block to filter light to the auditorium below.

an octagonal space enclosing the grand circular, domed reading room, called "one of the supreme examples of interior design in America" by the Landmarks Preservation Commission.

The richness of the interior begins in the vestibule beyond the bronze entry doors; it features sculptured stained-glass Tiffany windows and a floor of multicolored bands of mosaic tile. A narrow stairway with pale yellow marble walls, Portland stone sculptural accents, and a barrel-vaulted ceiling leads to the main floor landing, where doors open to reveal the eighty-foot-tall reading room rotunda. Said to have been inspired by that of the British Museum, the space combines rich materials with warm colors and extravagant details. It is encircled by sixteen thirty-foot-high columns of green Connemara marble with elaborate gilded Corinthian capitals executed by Tiffany Glass and Decorating Company. Above is a balcony with openwork metal railings that support life-size classical statues. Overhead, White used a Guastavino tile system to shape an intricately coffered dome sixty feet in diameter with a stained-glass oculus (now covered over). Around the perimeter, mezzanines hold tiers of bookcases, and openings provide access to rooms for each department. Offices are located on the main floor, and stairways descend to the auditorium on the basement level.

In 1921 the original entry doors were replaced by the bronze White Memorial Doors designed by Stanford White's son, Lawrence Grant White, with ornamental reliefs designed by sculptors who had worked with the architect.

As the university expanded, the library was relocated in 1968. The building, neglected for years, suffered from water leaks and pollution; an explosion in 1969 destroyed the auditorium and ruined its Tiffany window. In 1970, when Marcel Breuer was the supervising architect for the campus, the auditorium was rebuilt in modern style. But the rotunda was used only for special events.

In 1973 the campus was sold to the City University of New York and became home to Bronx Community College, but the Gould Memorial Library remained vacant. In 1996 the school, with city funds, retained Platt Byard Dovell to restore the auditorium, and in 2004, with Getty Trust funds for a master plan to preserve the campus, Easton Architects developed a conservation plan to bring the library back to life. FacadeMD oversaw repairs to the Tiffany windows and the ceiling and restored the original colors on the plaster finishes. Though its function is still limited, the Gould Memorial Library is among the most distinguished works of architecture in the city.

The coffered dome originally had an elaborate Tiffany glass oculus, which was covered with a white panel after it was damaged in the explosion. The current restoration of the building, now focused on structural repairs, will eventually replace it with a replica of the original.

Registry Room,
Ellis Island Main Building

1900

Ellis Island, Manhattan
Boring & Tilton
Interior designated 1993

Ellis Island is the symbol of a nation of immigrants and was, for more than twelve million of them, the first entry point into America. Today it is part of a museum and a memorial to those who came into the country between 1892 and 1924, when American embassies assumed responsibility for handling paperwork and visas.

The Bureau of Immigration was created in 1891 within the U.S. Treasury Department, which allocated funds for a facility in New York City, the port of entry for most immigrants. Ellis Island, a twenty-seven-acre government-owned island near the Statue of Liberty, purchased from New York State in 1808 as part of a harbor-defense system, was chosen as the location.

The main building of Ellis Island was the first major federal commission executed under the Tarsney Act of 1893, which allowed public buildings to be designed by private architects through design competitions, opening the door to higher quality architecture. The guidelines for the new facility were restrictive: it had to be simple but substantial, of brick with stone trim, fireproof, and allowing easy emergency access. Prominent firms including McKim, Mead & White and Carrère & Hastings submitted proposals, but the commission was awarded to the little-known New York firm of Boring & Tilton. Equally responsible for the final result was James Knox Taylor, supervising architect of the Treasury Department and a former employee of Cass Gilbert. Their design was critically praised, and won a Gold Medal at the 1900 Paris Exposition.

The Registry Room occupies the central portion of the building's second and third floors. It is almost two hundred feet long, one hundred feet wide, and sixty feet high, with a monumental vaulted ceiling, tiled floor and balcony and multi-paned, arched clerestory windows that admit copious natural light. A broad staircase provided access from the floor below, and iron railings separated the immigrants into lines as they waited to be processed. The column-free design solved the challenge of moving great numbers of people in and out—as many as 6,500 each day. The vast majority had traveled on steamships in

steerage, or third class—first- and second-class immigrants were usually admitted quickly, but those in the registry room were examined for physical ailments or contagious diseases before being granted entry.

The interior was altered as additional facilities were built; in 1911, the staircase was closed and the railings removed. The Guastavino tile barrel-vaulted ceiling and red herringbone-patterned Ludowici tile floor were added after damage from a 1916 saboteurs' attack.

Immigration through Ellis Island ended in 1924, and the facility was used for refugees, detainees and Coast Guard training until 1954. It was virtually abandoned until 1965, when President Lyndon Johnson made it part of the Statue of Liberty National Monument, overseen by the National Park Service. Yet this symbol of America's immigration heritage moldered for another decade. By the 1980s, when funds were allocated to stabilize the main building, holes in the roof were so big that snow was collecting on the floor and pigeons had taken up residence. The Registry Room opened to tourists on a limited basis but remained in a state of decay.

In 1993 the Landmarks Preservation Commission designated the interior of the main building and created the Ellis Island Historic District to protect other parts of the complex. Landmark designation came after what is said to be the largest historic restoration project in United States history. Beyer Blinder Belle Architects & Planners coordinated the transformation of the building into the Ellis Island Immigration Museum, rebuilding the stairway and retrofitting the interiors with theaters, a library, offices, and visitor amenities, as well as space for artifacts, oral histories, and media presentations.

During Hurricane Sandy in October 2012, the island was largely submerged. The museum reopened a year later, but much of the collection remains in storage, pending completion of new mechanical and electrical systems. The Registry Room is still the primary attraction, a resonant reminder of what generations of immigrants experienced during their first hours on American soil.

The Metropolitan Museum of Art

1902

1000 Fifth Avenue, Manhattan
Richard Morris Hunt, Richard Howland Hunt
George B. Post, consulting architect
Interior designated 1977

The Great Hall of the country's largest museum (over two million square feet), and one of the world's most prestigious, is a monumental Beaux-Arts space that serves as an introduction to the museum while providing an unforgettable experience for the crowds that pass through its doors.

Visitors ascend the Fifth Avenue staircase to the triple-arched vestibule, passing through a colonnade of fluted Ionic marble columns into a hall that is as grand as the institution. Clad in warm-toned Indiana limestone, the space is three stories high, with three circular domes supported by piers and arches. Circular skylights punctuate the domes, and a balcony with a pierced limestone railing wraps around the space. Deep niches, designed for statues and set off by sculpted ornament, punctuate the walls.

Within the museum, the Great Hall is the central space that orients visitors. The triple arch of the entry is mirrored across the hall with the portal to the grand staircase, which ascends to the second-floor galleries. At the ends of the long axis are openings marked by fluted Ionic columns leading to the first floor galleries on the north and south. Originally this axis extended through both wings. Today, with the atrium space in the Greek and Roman galleries, the axis has been restored to the south.

The idea of a national art institution was first articulated by John Jay, a prominent New York lawyer and a grandson of the country's first chief justice. Jay worked out the plans for the museum with an influential group of New Yorkers through the Union League Club. It was incorporated in 1870, and its first location was in the Dodsworth Building at 681 Fifth Avenue. It moved briefly to a mansion on West 14th Street before the current Central Park location was selected. The first structure on the site, completed in 1880, was a red brick Gothic Revival structure facing into the park. Now enclosed by subsequent expansions, the first building was designed by Calvert Vaux and Jacob Wrey

Mould, who had just completed the Museum of Natural History's first building.

Pressured by its expanding collections, the museum commissioned noted architect Richard Morris Hunt, a trustee and chairman of the building committee, to develop a master plan for expansion and to design a new structure that would face Fifth Avenue. In designing the new entrance wing, he followed examples set by the great museums of Europe, basing its classical form on Roman prototypes. After Hunt's death in 1895, his son Richard Howland Hunt completed the work, with consulting architect George B. Post.

Over the years, the grandeur of the Great Hall was diminished by interventions and expansions. In the late 1960s, the museum considered removing the grand staircase to facilitate access to the proposed Lehman Wing; fortunately, the staircase was left untouched. Many elements were restored in 1970 under the supervision of Kevin Roche John Dinkeloo and Associates, though critics protested the removal of the chandeliers in favor of uniform lighting, the openings in walls for expanded checkrooms and bookstores, the replacement of sculptures in the niches by floral arrangements, the installation of a massive information desk in the center of the hall, and the elimination of some of the decorative carving.

As part of the museum's ongoing expansion and maintenance, the Indiana limestone facade was cleaned in 2006 for the first time in its history, and the exterior fountains and staircase, which had been redone in 1970, were redesigned again in 2014, giving the Met another fresh face to present to visitors from all over the world.

New Amsterdam Theater

1903

Panels painted in the Art Nouveau style were an exception to the formality of the Beaux-Arts aesthetic of the time. The arches framing the walls and the proscenium are outlined by intricate plaster and carved oak moldings designed by Fritz and Max Neumark and modeled by St. John Issing.

214 West 42nd Street, Manhattan
Herts & Tallant
Interior designated 1997

The largest theater in New York when it was built, the New Amsterdam, along with the Lyceum Theater, is the oldest surviving Broadway-area venue. Its rescue is one of New York's great success stories. Spectacular in and of itself, it also stands as a symbol of the revival of 42nd Street and the entire Times Square theater district.

The New Amsterdam marked a significant innovation in design, as the first American theater to depart from the standard model of the European opera house, which favored elaborate and often overwhelming classical schemes. Instead, the architects turned to the more delicate Art Nouveau, a fashion-forward style that had become popular in Belgium and France but was rarely seen in the United States. Thanks to a meticulous and costly restoration, the New Amsterdam has again become a showcase of the style, one of its few examples in New York and, indeed, in the United States.

Commissioned by the impresarios Marcus Klaw and A. L. Erlanger, the theater was a costly and ambitious venture, employing the skills of an impressive roster of architects, sculptors, painters, and artisans. On its opening, the New Amsterdam was given a more enthusiastic review than the show it presented and was cited as establishing an example for other theater owners to follow.

The long, relatively narrow lobby introduces the Art Nouveau theme in curvilinear floral motifs on terra-cotta pilasters and sculptured panels depicting scenes from famous plays. Beyond the lobby, a broader entry leads to a promenade foyer and a reception room, both with groin-vaulted ceilings and similar foliate ornament. Marble stairs with decorative balustrades provide access to balconies and basement lounges.

The auditorium itself is a broad, elliptical space with curved walls, a domed ceiling, and two balconies, cantilevered to allow unobstructed views. This use of cantilevered construction in a theater was an innovation, credited to the architect Henry B. Herts. Intricately detailed oak moldings and plasterwork of vines, flowers, and peacocks decorate the walls, dome, and proscenium, and fantasy murals in a mélange of silvery green with

Above the proscenium is a mural by Robert Blum and Albert B. Wenzell representing allegorical figures related to drama.

The promenade foyer runs the width of the auditorium. The groin-vaulted ceiling has floral moldings with lily and lotus motifs and a color scheme complementing that of the auditorium.

An elliptical colonnade supports the domed ceiling in the lower-level New Amsterdam room. The bronze grille at the center of the dome depicts a winged youth by George da Maduro Peixotto.

muted pastel accents, depict allegorical representations of drama and the arts.

In addition to its extravagant decor, the New Amsterdam was technically advanced for its time. It had sophisticated heating, cooling, and vacuum cleaning systems, as well as fireproofing. Most unusual, the stage could be lowered two stories by a system of elevators and electric motors, and it had an electrical switchboard—advantages that made it well suited for elaborate shows. The theater opened in November 1903 with a production of Shakespeare's *A Midsummer Night's Dream*, and until 1927 it was host to the renowned Ziegfeld Follies. Later presentations included contemporary dramas and Shakespearean plays as well as operettas and musicals.

The financial pressures of the Depression battered many Broadway theaters, and the New Amsterdam was no exception. It went bankrupt and closed in 1937. A new owner converted it into a movie theater, removing

the auditorium boxes but otherwise leaving the interiors largely intact. A restoration effort in the 1980s stalled, resulting in further damage.

Hardy Holzman Pfeiffer was commissioned in 1992 by the State of New York, exercising its urban renewal authority, to stabilize and restore the virtually ruined interior. The spaces were transformed—almost every surface was replaced, and the colors, finishes, and decorative details were re-created—a sensitive facelift for the venerable site. The process took five years, strengthened by a partnership with the Walt Disney Company. Disney's investment, combined with public subsidies, energized the 42nd Street Development Project and gave Broadway back one of its crown jewels.

The New Amsterdam reopened on April 2, 1997, and since then has thrived as a venue for Disney productions of *The Lion King*, *Mary Poppins*, and *Aladdin*—all appropriate tenants for its fanciful interiors.

City Hall Station
IRT Transit System

1904

Rarely seen by subway riders even when it was in use, the ceiling vaults are outlined in geometrically patterned Guastavino tile. The largest skylight is still visible from City Hall Park, though the glass was painted black during World War II as protection from the threat of air raids.

Beneath City Hall Park, Manhattan
Heins & LaFarge
Designated 1979

Few New Yorkers—and even fewer visitors to the city—know about this extraordinary space, just steps away from the Brooklyn Bridge but many feet underground. Opened in the early years of the city subway system, it was the southern terminus of the "Manhattan Main Line" (now the Lexington Avenue line). As passenger traffic mushroomed over the years, the station outlived its usefulness, its sharply curved configuration unable to accommodate longer modern trains. It was closed and boarded up in 1945, a landmark made obsolete by progress.

By the mid-nineteenth century, the burgeoning population of New York City had generated appalling traffic congestion. An underground rapid transit system was proposed as early as the 1860s, but it was not until 1891 that the State Legislature formed a Rapid Transit

Commission to investigate the possibility. In 1899 the Rapid Transit Subway Construction Company, backed by banker August P. Belmont Jr., was contracted to build the city's first underground system. William Barclay Parsons, named chief engineer of the system, planned a route through Manhattan and into the Bronx, beginning under City Hall. Construction began in 1900 for what became the Interborough Rapid Transit Company (IRT), one of the city's original subway lines (the others are the BMT and the IND).

The City Hall station, as terminus of the line at the seat of the government, was conceived as unique. It is a richly colored showcase of tiled vaults and arches, brass chandeliers, and skylights, the largest of which is still embedded in City Hall Park. Although portions of twelve other stations on the line have been designated as interior landmarks, the City Hall station is generally acknowledged as the most exceptional in design.

The firm of Heins & LaFarge, selected for the IRT project by a search committee, was also responsible for the original designs of the Cathedral of St. John the Divine (where they had used similar decorative elements)

A series of elegant arches springing from the wainscot enhances the space, in keeping with the mandate of the City Beautiful movement.

and the New York Zoological Gardens (Bronx Zoo). For the subway system, they were assigned the design of the stations, kiosks, and control houses. Chief Engineer Parsons oversaw the planning and construction of the stations and probably influenced their design as well, as he had made a study of European transit systems and had approval over Heins & LaFarge's plans. The assignment imposed few restrictions, mandating walls of white or light-colored tiles or brick, but also requiring "painting and decoration to give brightness and cheerfulness to the general effect." Taking full advantage of the opportunity,

the architects conceived bold decorative schemes that, though clearly related from one station to another, gave each a distinctive identity through color and ornamental details. The most striking feature of the City Hall station is the high vaulted ceiling executed by the Guastavino Fireproof Construction Company. Some 50,000 glazed ochre-tone tiles form a series of herringbone-patterned vaults, each framed by bands of zig-zag patterned green and brown tiles, that follow the looping curve of the 240-foot-long platform. Leaded-glass skylights are set into three of the vaults and at the station entrance. The platforms are of poured concrete, and Roman brick wainscoting on the walls is capped with marble. Decorative brown, blue, and white faience plaques identify the station at fifteen-foot intervals.

When the City Hall station opened in October 1904, the owners were praised for their contribution

to public art. Over the years, however, City Hall, unlike other stations, was neither redesigned nor upgraded. In the late 1990s the Metropolitan Transportation Authority proposed to renovate the station as a branch of the New York City Transit Museum. Security issues quashed the idea, and there is scant likelihood of the station's reopening. Occasional tours are organized through the Transit Museum for its members, and interested subway riders can see the station through the windows of the downtown 6 train as it makes the turnaround to go back uptown.

Each station had its own distinctive tile signage.

A plaque commemorates the IRT, the city's first underground line.

Pierpont Morgan Library

1906

H. Siddons Mowbray's ceiling murals and decorative plasterwork were based on Renaissance prototypes, but his themes relate to the Morgan collections, depicting the ancient world, the Middle Ages, and the Renaissance. The lunette above the East Room entrance illustrates Arthurian romance, and others pay homage to poetry and Greek scholars.

Museum entrance: 225 Madison Avenue, Manhattan
McKim, Mead & White
Interior designated 1982

Built for one of the most prominent figures of the Gilded Age by the leading architectural firm of its time, the Morgan Library is a superb work of architecture, and a harmonious blend of exterior and interiors. The Renaissance Revival building contains an extraordinary ensemble of rooms that have been in continuous use, meticulously cared for, since its conversion from private facility to public museum nine decades ago.

John Pierpont Morgan was one of the most influential figures of the late nineteenth and early twentieth century. A banker, railroad financier, and organizer of U.S. Steel, Morgan was also a voracious collector. Beginning with early printed books and manuscripts, he expanded his interest to amass major collections of old master drawings and ancient Near Eastern seals that are among the treasures now housed in the library he built.

He was also a benefactor of the Metropolitan Museum of Art, serving as trustee and later president.

The patrician white marble library was built alongside Morgan's New York residence, an unpretentious brownstone at the corner of Madison Avenue and 36th Street, to accommodate the growing collections that had been divided between his residences in New York and London, and in storage. He hired the celebrated firm of McKim, Mead & White for the project.

The result, considered by many to be Charles McKim's finest work, is a majestic repository for Morgan's collections. Part library and part museum, its 14,700-square-foot interior interprets Renaissance Revival design in four different but aesthetically related rooms: an entrance hall, a study, a gallery, and the library proper. The entrance hall is an opulent vaulted rotunda with freestanding lapis lazuli columns, mosaic panels, and a varicolored marble floor in a pattern based on one in the Villa Pia in the Vatican gardens, executed by sculptor Thomas Waldo Story. American muralist H. Siddons Mowbray painted the lunettes and the domed ceiling in a style inspired by Raphael's ceiling in the Stanza della

Segnatura in the Vatican. The lunettes depict figures from ancient, medieval, and Renaissance poetry, reflecting one of the subjects in the library collections.

Mr. Morgan's study was designed by the French-born American decorator and muralist James Wall Finn, featuring red silk damask walls and upholstery, a carved marble fireplace, low bookcases, and an Italian wood ceiling, painted by Finn with Renaissance coats of arms. A portrait of Morgan hangs over the fireplace. At the opposite side of the Rotunda is the magnificent East Room, whose walls are lined with three tiers of bookcases, fronted with brass-grilled doors and densely packed with richly bound volumes. The vaulted ceiling and upper wall panels are painted with images of philosophers, Roman deities, artists, scientists, representations of the arts and sciences, and astrological signs. The paintings were done off-site; Mowbray worked for three

The half-dome of the apse is decorated with intricate plaster-work depicting figures of Greek mythology in relief on blue backgrounds.

years in his Greenwich Village studio, painting them on canvas, and finishing just in time for them to be installed in the completed building. The North Room, originally the librarian's office, is a gallery, lined with cases for Morgan's collection of ancient Near Eastern engraved seals and tablets.

In 1924 J. P. Morgan Jr. made the library a public institution, and it has since become an important addition to the city's roster of museums, housing treasures such as Gutenberg Bibles, illuminated manuscripts, original scores by celebrated classical composers like Beethoven and Verdi, and drawings by such artists as Leonardo da Vinci and Michelangelo. New acquisitions have required expansions, including a 1928 annex built on the site of Morgan's residence and the 1988 purchase of Morgan Jr.'s 37th Street brownstone. In 1991 Voorsanger & Mills connected the three buildings with an enclosed garden court, which was replaced in 2006 in a major expansion by Renzo Piano that included a three-story glass pavilion as well as new event and exhibition areas. Though controversial as an addition to the historic complex, the expansion left the original McKim building intact. A complete interior restoration by Beyer Blinder Belle Architects & Planners and new lighting by Renfro Design Group has renewed the luster of the original materials.

The original bronze entrance doors have long been closed, and the designated interiors are now accessed

Rich silk damask wallcovering in Morgan's study bears the coat of arms of the Chigi banking family, an eight-poointed star and mountain formation.

Overleaf: The East Room is dominated by three tiers of wood bookcases, crowned by a coffered ceiling with eighteen lunettes painted with murals by Mowbray, drawn from examples in the Villa Farnesina. In the spandrels, he depicted Zodiac symbols and Roman deities.

from the new wing through modern glass doors, but their impact on visitors has not been reduced. Now the Morgan Library and Museum, the building and its exceptional interiors are a reminder of the lavishness of Gilded Age style, of Morgan's obsessive collecting and his commitment to provide a showcase for his treasures for future generations to enjoy.

Behind the East Room mantel is a sixteenth-century tapestry of *The Triumph of Avarice* from the series The Seven Deadly Sins designed by Pieter Coecke van Aelst.

The North Room, originally the office of the librarian, now holds Morgan's collection of ancient Near Eastern seals and tablets. On the mantel is a bronze bust of the Italian poet Boccaccio.

The vault off Mr. Morgan's study.

United States Custom House

1907

The grandest space in the Custom House, the Collector's Office is a showpiece of Renaissance Revival ornament, with a massive stone fireplace and a spectacular Tiffany carved-wood screen.

One Bowling Green, Manhattan
Cass Gilbert
Interior designated 1979

These majestic interiors are housed in an imposing building designed by one of the leading architects of the early twentieth century. Situated prominently at the foot of Broadway, the Beaux-Arts structure was designed to house America's oldest federal agency, the United States Customs Service, which oversaw the collection of tariffs on imports. Through a combination of public and private efforts, the former Custom House, like Ellis Island and Federal Hall, has been successfully reborn.

The Customs Service, established in 1789, had been located in the building now known as Federal Hall, and then in the Merchants' Exchange at 55 Wall Street. Gilbert's design, selected from among twenty submissions, was built under the provision of the Tarsney Act, which allowed architectural competitions for the design of federal buildings. It was an important commission, since before the establishment of income tax, customs

duties were a key source of government revenue, and New York was the country's leading port. The new building, officially named the Alexander Hamilton U.S. Custom House, was built on land the government had purchased in 1892, on the site of the city's first custom house, which had burned down in 1815.

Cass Gilbert was well established by the time he received the commission. He had worked for McKim, Mead & White, and though he designed the Gothic-inspired Woolworth and New York Life Buildings, his most celebrated works, including the U.S. Supreme Court building, followed classical tradition.

The seven-story Custom House covers an impressive expanse of three square blocks. To make it even more prominent, Gilbert chose to face the building toward the city, rather than the expected orientation to the harbor and the arriving ships. The grand staircase on Bowling Green, flanked by sculptures of four continents by Daniel Chester French, leads to a barrel-vaulted transverse lobby that opens onto the two-story Great Hall. An opulent introduction to the expansive interior, it is lined with monumental marble columns supporting an elaborate entablature and tall arches. The floor displays

geometrically patterned multicolored marble. At either end, freestanding staircases rise to the upper floors.

Arches frame the entry into the central and most impressive part of the interior, the elliptical Rotunda crowned with a dome built using the Guastavino structural system, providing a lightweight but exceptionally strong support for the 140-ton glass and metal skylight. The dome was undecorated until 1937, when the Treasury Relief Art Project, an offshoot of the Depression-era Works Progress Administration, commissioned artist Reginald Marsh to paint a series of murals. He and eight assistants filled 2,300 square feet of space with frescoes depicting early explorers and modern shipping scenes in New York harbor.

At the front of the building, separated from the other working areas, is the Collector's Office, an appropriately impressive interior signifying the status of its powerful

Between the paneled walls and the polychrome ceiling in the Collector's Office are a series of paintings of seventeenth-century ports by Elmer E. Garnsey, who also painted the ceiling mural at the Library of Congress.

The ceiling of the entry hall is adorned with paintings by Garnsey.

occupant. Encased in oak from inlaid floor to paneled walls to ornately coffered and decorated ceiling, it is dominated by an elaborately carved fireplace. In the center is a Renaissance-style carved-wood screen by Tiffany Studios. Paintings of seventeenth-century ports by Elmer E. Garnsey line the walls. Here and throughout the interiors of the building, nautical ornament pays tribute to the city as a seaport.

After the relocation of the Customs Service in 1971, the building stood empty, its future endangered, until

A clock marks the joint between the entrance hall and the rotunda.

The oval dome in the rotunda is surrounded by paintings by Reginald Marsh of famous explorers and shipping scenes in New York harbor.

a group of Lower Manhattan business leaders partnered with the city and federal government to restore the exterior and interiors. The Custom House reopened for the 1976 Bicentennial as the site of a series of cultural events, but then the building sat vacant again while the General Services Administration, which owns and manages the property, sought proposals for transforming it into a cultural institution.

Funds were finally authorized by Congress, and Ehrenkrantz Eckstut & Kuhn Architects oversaw a decade-long restoration. Completed in 1994, it included the cleaning and conservation of murals, woodwork, metalwork, and marble, and adapting part of the building to house the U.S. Bankruptcy Court and National Museum of the American Indian, which opened that year, making the grand interiors once more accessible to the public. In 2001 the rotunda was restored and is again the showpiece of the building. Since 2012 the National Archives at New York City are also headquartered there, providing access for scholars and organizing exhibitions within the historic space.

The Plaza Hotel

1907, 1921, 1929

768 Fifth Avenue
Henry J. Hardenbergh, Warren & Wetmore, and
Schultze & Weaver
Interior designated 2005

One of the oldest and perhaps the best known of New York's luxury hotels, The Plaza has welcomed guests for more than a century. Its legendary public spaces, designed by three different architecture firms in a variety of extravagant styles, have been reimagined for a modern clientele, as nostalgic reminders of gracious living in an earlier, elegant age.

As the twentieth century dawned, Fifth Avenue was becoming a street of luxury shops, accessible to the mansions facing the East side of Central Park. The Plaza, built where the two areas met, replaced a fifteen-year-old hotel of the same name, and was largely the concept of hotelier Frederic Sterry, who managed it until 1932. He envisioned a world-class venue outstripping everything in the city—and even the country. The ambitious project took two years and cost $12 million, an unprecedented amount at the time.

Henry Hardenbergh was an appropriate architect for the project. He had designed elite hotels and apartment houses, including the landmark Dakota Apartments (1884) and the original Waldorf and Astoria hotels (both now demolished), and his ability to translate historicist styles into spaces that were both picturesque and comfortable set the standard for luxury hotels.

The chateau-like Plaza (almost a skyscraper when it was built) is an imposing presence, and its major public areas, all of which are designated landmarks, are the key to its success. Each space has its own character, but they merge seamlessly into a harmonious ensemble.

The original main lobby, facing Central Park, was conceived by Hardenbergh as a cream-and-white Beaux-Arts space with white and Breccia marble stonework. The Oak Room's German Renaissance Revival interior, by L. Alavoine & Company, had carved oak paneling, a barrel-vaulted ceiling, and murals of medieval castles framing the bar. Carved reliefs and a grape-festooned chandelier referenced the role of the original men-only

The Fifth Avenue lobby, designed
by Hardenburgh, was the original
entrance to the hotel.

drinking space. The Edwardian Room, decorated by
William Baumgarten & Co. in Spanish Renaissance
Revival style, featured oak wainscoting and an elabo-
rately stenciled, trussed-and-mirrored ceiling.

The Palm Court, an airy, skylit tea room that became
the archetype for similar spaces around the country, was
designed by E. Spencer Hall & Company and interior decorator John Smeraldi as a neoclassical fantasy, with marble
columns, mirrored walls, and tall casement windows. Its
most prominent ornament, apart from the trees that gave
the room its name, were life-size marble caryatids representing the four seasons, designed by Pottier & Stymus.

Almost every item in the hotel was custom made,
including 1,650 crystal chandeliers and the largest-ever
order of gold-rimmed dinnerware. Half of the guests
would be long-term residents; for many affluent New
Yorkers, living in a hotel with modern amenities like

electricity, central heating, elevators, and a large service
staff was preferable to maintaining a townhouse. When
the Plaza opened on October 1, 1907, Alfred Gwynne
Vanderbilt Sr. and his family were the first guests.

In 1921 Warren & Wetmore added the neoclassical
Fifth Avenue lobby and the three-level neo-Renaissance
Terrace Room, with elaborate decor by Smeraldi. Schultze
& Weaver, the preeminent hotel architects who had
designed several Biltmores, the Breakers in Palm Beach,
and the landmark Waldorf-Astoria, added the vast
Grand Ballroom in 1929. The white and gold interior
had an ornate coved ceiling and two levels of balconies.

The translucent glass ceiling with lattice and foliate decoration creates an airy, outdoor atmosphere in the Palm Court.

Murals of medieval castles are interspersed with elaborately carved paneling in the Oak Room.

Several changes in ownership led to transformations of the public rooms. In 1943 Hilton renovated the Fifth Avenue lobby, replaced the Palm Court skylight, and opened the Oak Bar, with Tudor Revival interiors credited to the architect Frederick P. Platt and murals by Everett Shinn. After Hilton sold the hotel in 1953, the Grand Ballroom—site of Truman Capote's famous 1966 Black and White Ball—was "updated" with new colors, and the Edwardian Room was transformed with a much-criticized garden scheme. Landmark designation in 1969 protected the hotel exterior, but the interiors could not be included at that time. As new owners, Westin undertook restoration in 1974 to reverse the unfortunate changes.

Under Donald Trump's ownership from 1988 to 1995, the Plaza interiors were again redecorated. In 2004, the hotel was sold once more, and closed for renovation. Many of the furnishings were dispersed at an on-site "tag sale" and a Christie's auction in 2006. When plans were announced to convert the hotel to mixed residential and commercial use, public concern and protests by the hotel workers' union helped win Mayor Michael Bloomberg's support for interior landmark status. Part of the Plaza remains a hotel, part has been converted into condominiums, and an underground retail complex has been added.

The latest renovation, approved by the LPC, has been more reinterpretation than restoration. Gal Nauer Architects developed the master plan and Walter B. Melvin Architects oversaw the restorations, and over the past several years, the legendary interiors have gradually reopened. Though not precisely as they were originally, the Plaza's public rooms recall the glamour of its original incarnation, one of the few remaining mementos of New York's Gilded Age.

Surrogate's Court

1907

One of a pair of massive piers topped with monumental scrolls and intricately detailed carving that mark the base of the grand staircase.

Overleaf: The main lobby is an enclosure of golden Siena marble, framed by an arcaded gallery and carved with classical ornament.

31 Chambers Street, Manhattan
John R. Thomas, Horgan & Slattery
Interior designa ed 1976

Behind the monumental but relatively severe facade of Surrogate's Court are a series of grandiose interiors exemplifying Gilded Age opulence to a degree rarely seen in civic architecture. The design was originally intended for a building to replace New York's City Hall in the 1890s. When public outcry put an end to that project, the plans found another life as the Hall of Records, part of the civic center complex around City Hall Park. The Landmarks Preservation Commission, in designating five floors of the interior as well as the exterior, described it as a "magnificent architectural symbol of the prosperity, importance, and achievement of New York City."

John R. Thomas, the architect, was a prominent designer of public buildings, and his submission was chosen from 133 entries in the competition for the design of a new City Hall. He revised the plans to include a depository of court records, and construction of the Hall of Records began in 1899. After Thomas's death in 1901, the politically connected firm of Horgan & Slattery was appointed as architects. Their names appear with Thomas's on the cornerstone, although Thomas's original design was essentially retained, and it is for this building that he is best known.

Above the triple-arched entrance of the seven-story Maine granite building are eight thirty-six-foot-high Corinthian columns, built on a steel frame for fire resistance—a critical factor in the protection of city records. Though the exterior gives no hint of the extravagance within, the entry foyer, running along the front of the building, heralds the spectacle to come. Its vault is covered with multicolored ceramic- and glass-tile mosaics depicting stylized ancient deities and zodiac symbols. Mosaics in a more narrative style also enhance the soffits and reveals of the double mahogany doors at each end of the foyer. The artist for both, William de Leftwich Dodge, also worked on the Algonquin Hotel, the New York State Capitol in Albany, and other public sites. Above the doors sit marble sculptures by Albert Weinert, whose work is also seen in the Library of Congress.

In the entry hall, the arched ceiling by artist William de Leftwich Dodge is a series of ceramic-and-glass-tile mosaics depicting ancient dieties and symbols of the zodiac.

The engaged columns and balustrade of the upper arcade contrast with the massive rusticated piers below.

The main lobby is a majestic expanse of honey-colored Siena marble walls, pink-and-beige marble floor, and an elliptically arched bronze ceiling with a vaulted skylight. The building extends three more stories around the open space above. A palatial staircase, adorned with high-relief scrolls, garlands, and other carved ornament, leads to an arcaded gallery on the second floor. The upper levels, accessed by additional marble staircases, are given distinctive and equally elaborate decorative treatments. The hallways on the third through fifth floors circle an interior courtyard with walls of gray-veined marble, and floors of mosaic tile bordered with a Greek fret pattern. Despite its monumental scale, the warm colors and rich ornamentation make the space more welcoming than intimidating.

The fifth floor houses the Surrogate's Court: two symmetrically planned courtrooms, one finished in mahogany with a paneled ceiling featuring classical, high-relief bronzed ornament, the other in English oak with a paneled ceiling decorated with high-relief gilded ornament.

Denoting its primary function, the building was originally named the Hall of Records and the Surrogate's Court was a tenant, but in 1962 it was renamed after the court. To secure the future of the extraordinary space despite changes in its use, the Landmarks Preservation Commission designated the interior in 1976. More recently, Swanke Hayden Connell Architects restored the exterior and the second-floor offices, making necessary repairs, reversing inappropriate changes, and concealing infrastructure improvements to maintain the integrity of the building and its spectacular interiors.

Belasco Theater

1907

The meticulous restoration of the Belasco included rebuilding the boxes and restoring the Tiffany stained-glass ceiling panels and light fixtures.

111 West 44th Street, Manhattan
George Keister
Interior designated 1987

A star of the Broadway theater district, the Belasco is a showpiece of its architectural genre and a monument to the impresario for whom it was named. As one of the oldest and smallest Broadway theaters, it was also among the most endangered interiors in New York. Today it wears its age beautifully, thanks to a restoration that repaired damages and replicated lost elements of its warm and inviting spaces.

David Belasco, called the "Bishop of Broadway" for his habit of wearing clerical garb, was a visionary whose ideas helped transform the theatergoing experience. The first decades of the twentieth century saw an explosion of new venues, most of which followed the model of the European opera house: a high proscenium, narrow auditorium, and two or three horseshoe-shaped balconies with dozens of boxes, designed in a cornucopia of styles. Belasco pioneered what became the American Little Theater

movement, fostering a more intimate exchange between actors and audience in an environment that suggested the living room of a private home. The Belasco was the laboratory for his experiments, an archetype for American theaters in integrating exterior and interior, and the first of a dozen more to be designed by its architect.

Built at the then-extravagant cost of $750,000, the theater was originally called the Stuyvesant, since Belasco already had a namesake location on 42nd Street (now the New Victory), but it was renamed in 1910. With just over one thousand seats and no obstructing columns, it offers the intimacy Belasco sought: the orchestra seating was wider than it was deep, with a shallow balcony and gallery above, bringing the audience closer to the stage. Equally important, the decor was not extravagantly baroque but a restrained blend of styles more often associated with residential interiors.

The lobby suggests a Tyrolean castle, with wood paneling and murals. It opens onto the richly colored auditorium, a melange of neoclassical and rococo styles whose primary decorative elements are Tiffany glass and a series of eighteen murals by Everett Shinn on the walls and over the proscenium arch. The romantic

images complement the red and gold color scheme, enhanced by diffused lighting, filtered through stained and leaded panels of Tiffany glass in distinctive octagonal light fixtures and hanging lanterns. Tiffany glass also appears on decorative wall and ceiling panels, and ornamental capitals of the columns supporting the balcony and the pilasters flanking the boxes.

The domestic atmosphere was the perfect setting for the intimate dramas for which the theater was designed. When it opened in 1907, the Stuyvesant/Belasco was hailed as the most beautiful theater in the city. But Belasco's concerns went beyond aesthetics; his innovative technology included diffused lighting to enhance the ambience and a stage that lowered to facilitate set changes.

After acquiring the theater in 1948, the Shubert Organization adapted the interior to various entertainments, including an NBC radio playhouse from 1949 to 1953. It returned to theatrical productions in 1953 and has remained in use ever since. Its best-known productions were *Oh! Calcutta!* (1971) and *The Rocky Horror Show* (1975), but it has presented Shakespearean plays and classical revivals as well.

With the advent of large-scale musical spectacles, small theaters like the Belasco suffered, and some even closed. The 1982 destruction of the Helen Hayes and Morosco Theaters for construction of a Times Square hotel ignited a five-year battle to save Broadway theaters, as much for their cultural significance as for their aesthetic appeal. In 1985 the Landmarks Preservation Commission conducted public hearings on more than forty theaters, in alphabetical order. Over the protests of owners who argued that their theaters needed constant change to accommodate an ever-evolving art form, the Belasco and twenty-five of its neighbors were designated in 1987. Despite lawsuits, the designations prevailed in exchange for important policy change. The LPC passed special theater guidelines allowing interior alterations as long as they are reversible, and the City Planning Commission passed a zoning provision making it easier for theater owners to sell valuable air rights and use part of the proceeds to fund new productions.

By the time the Shubert Organization undertook a sensitive restoration to celebrate the theater's centennial, some fixtures had been removed, others were damaged or lost, and some of the murals had been overpainted. The restoration, overseen by architect Francesca Russo and completed in 2010, became an arduous reclamation project: fixtures were refurbished or re-created; murals were cleaned and inappropriate overpainting removed; molds were crafted to replicate original plasterwork;

stained-glass elements were replaced, cleaned, or repaired and reassembled. After years of wear, some elements needed total replacement; new seats, upholstery, and carpets were designed to complement the motifs and colors of the decor. A balcony entrance, once used to separate the classes of theatergoers, was eliminated, and modern amenities were installed.

Reviving the Belasco, and the theater district around it, owes much to the concurrent improvement of the Times Square area as a whole. Happily, the Belasco interior today reflects David Belasco's goal of providing his audiences with an intimate and visually satisfying theater experience.

Two shallow balconies create a more intimate space than that of the traditional horseshoe-configuration.

Dime Savings Bank

1908, 1918, 1932

Medallions bearing the Mercury figure from the dime, the minimum deposit for a savings account, are inset on all of the capitals of the central columns, and on the frieze beneath the dome.

9 DeKalb Avenue, Brooklyn
Mowbray & Uffinger, Walker & Ward, Halsey, McCormack & Helmer
Interior designated 1994

At a time when grand banking floors have been made superfluous by mergers, online transactions, and cash machines, the Dime Savings Bank has been a rare and beautiful anachronism. While most of the monumental banking structures built in the early years of the twentieth century were converted to other uses, the Dime retained its original function and its remarkable interior, though it, too, is about to change.

The banking floor of the Dime echoes the irregular shape of the imposing pedimented building, at the intersection of two avenues. Almost triangular, with 160-foot-long sides and squared-off corners, the interior is an unexpected and spectacular contrast of classical forms and glorious color, with expanses of colored marble and polychrome painted decoration. Anchoring the space, ten towering red marble columns support a soaring blue-painted dome and enclose a three-faced bronze clock set royally on a tall black marble pedestal. Marble tellers' stations line the perimeter, and balconies with marble balustrades overlook the space. The floor is an intricate pattern of multicolored marble stars and hexagons, motifs repeated on the coffered ceiling. Railings, doors, and chandeliers are of polished bronze, and many incorporate the front and back of the "Mercury" dime, the bank's symbol since its founding in 1859.

The elaborate interior, said to have been inspired in part by Stanford White's design for the Bowery Savings Bank, was an expansion of the Dime's original modest facility, intended to assert the bank's stature in a period of unprecedented growth. At the turn of the twentieth century, savings banks, a relatively new type of institution, were seeking to attract depositors with the promise of trustworthiness and stability. Design became an effective means of conveying those qualities, through stately but inviting environments in residential neighborhoods. Classicism, more than any other style, connoted both respectability and security; the desirable qualities sought for government buildings and cultural institutions were equally appropriate for banks. The Dime became the

Marble benches, inscribed with quotations from *Poor Richard's Almanac,* are inserted between the columns. The hexagonal pattern of the coffered ceiling is repeated on the polychrome marble floor.

Pierced metal doors in the entrance foyer lead to an adjacent hallway.

The four-faced copper-and-bronze clock in the center of the banking hall.

The brass bases of the check-writing tables also incorporate images of Mercury.

busiest savings bank in Brooklyn, and for a time was the only one with more than one branch.

As real estate became more valuable and changes in banking practices reduced the need for large facilities, most of the grand bank structures were abandoned in favor of smaller ones. By the 1990s, the Landmarks Preservation Commission began to protect this category of interior and, as it had done earlier with theaters, created special parameters to streamline the process of adapting them.

Having been in continual use for its original function, the Dime interiors are largely intact, despite concessions to automated banking, and a change in ownership—the Dime became a Chase branch, one of few surviving reminders of an era when going to a bank could be a special occasion. Its time, however, was limited. Chase moved out in May 2015. The building is being sold, and under new ownership, is likely to be repurposed for another use.

New York Public Library

1911

476 Fifth Avenue, Manhattan
Carrère & Hastings
Interior designated 1974

The approach to the main branch of the New York Public Library (officially the Steven A. Schwarzman Building), past the celebrated lion statues and up the grand staircase into the ceremonial entrance hall, is a fitting introduction to one of the country's greatest research institutions. Its principal public spaces—Astor Hall and the McGraw Rotunda—were the first in New York to receive designation as landmark interiors.

By the late nineteenth century, New York was a major commercial metropolis and sought to become a cultural center as well. A great museum had been built, and a great library was another necessity. In 1895 two existing smaller libraries—the Astor and the Lenox—were combined with a bequest from former governor Samuel J. Tilden to form the New York Public Library. The site of the Croton Reservoir at 42nd Street and Fifth Avenue was chosen for the new library. It took two years to demolish the reservoir and another nine to construct the library. The largest marble structure built in America at the time, it remains a masterpiece of Beaux-Arts design.

As was customary for public buildings, a design competition was held for the prestigious commission, drawing scores of entries from the country's leading architectural firms. The winners, John Merven Carrère and Thomas Hastings, were little known at the time. Both were graduates of the École des Beaux-Arts and had worked at McKim, Mead & White. The library commission brought them national prominence, though Carrère died in 1911, and the firm's later skyscrapers, like the Cunard and the Standard Oil Buildings, were designed without him.

The imposing main lobby, later named Astor Hall after John Jacob Astor, one of the institution's chief benefactors, is a huge space, more than seventy feet long, forty-four feet wide, and thirty-four feet high, clad in creamy white Vermont Danby marble. The three arches of the portico are supported by columns, as are the facing arches, which open into corridors on the first and second floors. The barrel-vaulted ceiling is framed in garlands and rosettes, and the floor of Siena and Haute-

McGraw Rotunda

One of four murals by Laning representing the evolution of the written word, which are set into shallow bays in the walls of the McGraw Rotunda.

A profusion of classical motifs enhances the gilded and poly-chrome ceiling.

Grand marble stairs ascend to the second floor with views back into Astor Hall through arched openings.

ville marble is geometrically patterned with alternating squares and circles-in-squares. At each end of the hall, a marble staircase with a stone balustrade leads to the upper floors; niches on the landings contain busts of the architects.

The third-floor central hall, later named the McGraw Rotunda, is a grand rectangular space, with arched bays more than seventeen feet high, and walnut walls carved with Corinthian pilasters above a varicolored marble base. In 1940 and 1942, prominent painter Edward Laning, under the auspices of the Works Progress Administration,

painted murals depicting the history of the written word in bays in the paneled wall and on the barrel-vaulted ceiling. The hall leads to the Rose Reading Room—a universally admired interior omitted from landmark designation because trustees of the library wanted to retain the option of altering this most-used space.

The library was an immediate critical and popular success. The building was dedicated on May 23, 1911, and when it opened to the public the following day, more than 30,000 visitors crowded its halls. Despite its commanding presence, its importance as an architectural

A grand vaulted space, Astor Hall is at once magnificent and welcoming, with arched openings that beckon visitors further into the interior.

masterpiece was long undervalued, particularly as interest in classicism waned with the advent of modernism. Fortunately, that has changed in recent years

Over the years, Davis Brody Bond has overseen interior restoration and underground expansion of the library, including the meticulous restoration of the Rose Reading Room in 1998. A 2008 grant enabled a major restoration of the exterior that was completed in time for the library's 2011 centennial celebration.

Still a vital resource for researchers, the library has, in recent years, faced the challenge of updating its facilities to accommodate the increase in online research and other activities generated by the Internet. But an extensive expansion and renovation plan, announced in 2012, met with widespread public protest and lawsuits; its execution would have involved moving books to off-site storage in New Jersey and demolishing seven floors of stacks (a decision that the Landmarks Preservation Commission did not weigh in on because the stacks are not technically accessible to the public). Library officials abandoned the plan in May 2014 as too costly, and are seeking alternative means of expanding the venerable institution's role as a repository for books to one with facilities for the digital age as well.

Woolworth Building

1913

The interior of what was once the tallest building in the world is appropriately grand, with a vaulted mosaic ceiling above a Gothic-style stone frieze.

---

233 Broadway, Manhattan
Cass Gilbert
Interior designated 1983

One of the most important skyscrapers of its time and the last built before World War I, the "Cathedral of Commerce," as it was called, was originally, at 792 feet, the tallest structure in the world except for the Eiffel Tower, and the tallest in the city until 1930, when it was surpassed by 40 Wall Street, the Chrysler Building, and the Empire State in quick succession. The Woolworth Building remains the most prominent example of neo-Gothic architecture in New York, incorporating elements of the modern skyscraper in an unusual, four-sided design.

The building was designed as a monument to Frank W. Woolworth's empire of five-and-dime stores, and became an American icon and an international institution, but it was paid for—in cash—out of the millionaire's own pocket. He purchased and tore down five existing buildings on the corner of Park Place and Broadway and hired the eminent architect Cass Gilbert, who conceived an interior that, as the Landmarks Preservation Commission stated, "has rarely been equaled since, in New York or elsewhere." Like many others in his field, Gilbert began his career at McKim, Mead & White. His other celebrated works include the classical U.S. Custom House in New York and Supreme Court Building in Washington, D.C., but his use of the Gothic idiom in the Woolworth reflects his client's admiration of London's Houses of Parliament.

The configuration of the first floor does suggest a cruciform plan: it is a two-story arcade, twenty feet high and fifteen feet wide, formed by two intersecting barrel-vaulted corridors with a shallow dome at the crossing. The first corridor runs east–west from the principal entrance on Broadway to a grand marble stair hall, a large square space with a colored glass skylight. The central staircase led to the mezzanine offices of Irving Bank, a major tenant. The other corridor runs north–south, connecting the secondary entrances, and incorporating the elevator halls. The complex plan created separate access, and the decorative scheme provided individual identities, for the Woolworth Company and the bank. Beneath the mezzanine, the east–west

116

The monumental effect of the space is achieved through proportions, with exceptionally tall and narrow passages extending from the center of the lobby to entrances on Broadway and Park Place.

The broad marble staircase in the center of the lobby created a separate entrance area for the Irving Bank, a tenant and an investor in the building.

passage of the arcade was lined with shops, an unprecedented idea at the time that was later adopted in other skyscrapers. The arcade walls are clad in richly veined, vari-colored marble, quarried on the Greek island of Skyros, and crested with an elaborate Gothic-style carved stone cornice. The barrel-vaulted ceilings are covered with multicolored glass mosaics in an intricate abstract floral pattern recalling Byzantine design. Bronze Gothic-style tracery adorns the elevator doors, mailboxes, even the directories, with the initial "W" entwined with the ornament. Sculpted grotesques on the stonework and painted triptychs by Paul Jenewein depicting Labor and Commerce complete a decorative scheme far more elaborate than was customary for office buildings. The design was a glorification of commerce paying homage to the men responsible: at the mezzanine level, carved images by caricaturist Tom Johnson portray Woolworth and Gilbert, as well as the bank president, the engineer, the builder, even the rental agent.

Distinguished by its height and by the fact that it was ornamented on all four sides, the Woolworth Building became one of the most recognizable structures in the city. It was occupied by its original owners for more than seventy years, during which time it was carefully maintained with only minor additions such as modern light fixtures and telephone boxes on the walls. The Landmarks Preservation Commission considered the Woolworth Building for landmark status as early as 1970, but no vote was taken. Appreciating the building's architectural and historic significance, the Woolworth Company completed a major rehabilitation of the exterior in 1982 with the help of government subsidies, and the company, which had maintained the property without legal incentives, was persuaded to accept landmark designation for both the exterior and the lobby interiors to protect the building in case of a change in ownership.

In 1998 the building was sold, and Beyer Blinder Belle Architects & Planners was retained to renovate the exterior. After the 9/11 attacks, security protocol made the lobby virtually inaccessible to the public, except on organized tours. In 2012 the owners sold the upper thirty floors for conversion into luxury condominiums, maintaining the lower twenty-eight as offices, repurposing Woolworth's "Cathedral of Commerce" as a modern mixed-use facility.

On the balconies overlooking the entrance hall are painted panels with allegorical figures of Commerce (shown) and Labor.

Near the elevators, on a carved corbel is a caricature of Woolworth counting coins.

Della Robbia Bar

1913

4 Park Avenue, Manhattan
Warren & Wetmore
Interior designated 1994

A survivor from the early decades of the twentieth century, the Della Robbia Bar is notable for its vaulted ceiling and bold use of decorative ceramics by the Rookwood Pottery Company, one of the most celebrated firms of the American Arts and Crafts movement. Still in use as a restaurant, the Della Robbia Bar is the lone remnant of an interior ensemble destroyed in a 1960s modernization of the former Vanderbilt Hotel into a multi-use building.

The grotto-like space, nicknamed The Crypt, occupied a section of the base of the hotel built by millionaire sportsman Alfred Gwynne Vanderbilt near Grand Central Station, another Vanderbilt project, which was just being completed by architects Warren & Wetmore. The hotel, where Vanderbilt lived until he died in the sinking of the *Lusitania* in 1915, was part of his family's ambitious Terminal City project to develop the area east of Grand Central Station with buildings along Park Avenue, a

project that anticipated ideas later implemented in the creation of Rockefeller Center.

Though the exterior of the building is relatively restrained, divergent elements like extravagant terra-cotta lions' heads on the parapet, the vaulted lobby, and the ceramic-embellished restaurant made it more eclectic in execution. The fanciful decoration of the below-ground Della Robbia (divided into the cavernous, two-story Grill Room, an adjacent gallery, and the one-story balcony-level bar) was by Giovanni Battista Smeraldi (known as John Smeraldi), an Italian painter and decorator who worked on the interiors of many hotels, including the Plaza in New York and the Biltmore in Los Angeles.

The spaces were named for the Della Robbia family of Florentine sculptors, whose painted and glazed terra-cotta panels were widely admired. Dominating the interior of the bar is a Guastavino-tile vaulted ceiling (similar to the Oyster Bar in Grand Central), a network of nine curving bays formed by tan salt-glazed interlocking ceramic tiles in a herringbone pattern. Covering the soffits and trimming the ceiling arches are bands of colorful glazed tiles and architectural terra-cotta by the Rookwood Company of Cincinnati. The vaults are bordered in blue

and aqua tiles, with sculptured rosettes, ivory molding, and panels of yellow, green, and red. On the arch faces, a blue background sets off sculpted ivory-colored tile in a foliate pattern. The bar space opens onto two gallery bays that were once part of the Grill Room.

The Vanderbilts sold the hotel in 1925, and over the years its glamour faded, affected by a general decline in the hotel business. In the rush to modernize many buildings and interiors in the 1950s and 1960s, much of the terra-cotta ornament on the exterior was removed. In 1967, new owners converted the upper floors to apartments and the lower ones to commercial space, and most of the two-story Grill Room was converted into a parking garage. The remaining sections escaped demolition, though the original tile-encrusted columns were encased in wood and copper. Landmark designation for the surviving space came only when a grassroots campaign to save it was mounted by the Friends of Terra Cotta after the destruction of the Marine Grill, an equally exceptional terra-cotta interior at the nearby Hotel McAlpin. The Della Robbia Bar, incorporating part of the Grill Room gallery, is mostly intact and well maintained, now as Wolfgang's Steakhouse.

The blue and white Rookwood tiles on the ceiling vaults enliven the windowless bar.

The intricately detailed floral ornament tile is an unusual example of the work of the firm, which is best known for its Arts and Crafts ceramics.

Apollo Theater

1914

Within the monumental arches flanking the proscenium are two levels of double-tiered boxes. Elaborate gilded plasterwork featuring rococo arabesques and garlands covers the face of the arches.

253 West 125th Street, Manhattan
George Keister
Interior designated 1983

As much a cultural landmark as an architectural one, the Apollo was, for four decades, the country's most prominent showplace for African American entertainers. Its flamboyant marquee and colorful restored interior recall the history of burlesque and vaudeville shows, and the celebrated performers whose careers began there. Revived as a vital part of a reinvigorated, multicultural Harlem, it remains a symbol of those legendary years and the community it served.

The Apollo operated for two decades as Hurtig & Seamon's New Burlesque Theater, catering to white patrons in an era when blacks were not permitted to attend or perform. Celebrated burlesque promoter Billy Minsky took it over from 1928 until his death in 1932. Soon thereafter, mayor-to-be Fiorello La Guardia launched a campaign against burlesque and the theater closed down briefly, reopening in 1934 under new management as the Apollo. Burlesque shows were replaced by variety revues featuring leading black entertainers and targeted primarily at Harlem's burgeoning black community. Headliners included such legendary figures as jazz musicians Duke Ellington and Count Basie, dancer Bill "Bojangles" Robinson, singers Ray Charles and Aretha Franklin, and many others. Ella Fitzgerald and Jimi Hendrix were winners of the famed weekly Amateur Nights, and entertainers not welcome elsewhere, including Sammy Davis Jr., James Brown, Dionne Warwick, Stevie Wonder, and Mariah Carey, began their careers at the Apollo.

The years before World War II have come to be known as the Harlem Renaissance, when the neighborhood was the cultural capital of black America, with 125th Street at its heart and the Apollo its cornerstone. The theater's interiors, despite interim remodelings in the 1930s and 1950s that removed many decorative details, are still essentially as they were during its heyday, with much of the original neoclassical ornamental plasterwork intact.

The modern lobby leads into the 1,700-seat auditorium, consisting of a sloping, fan-shaped orchestra with

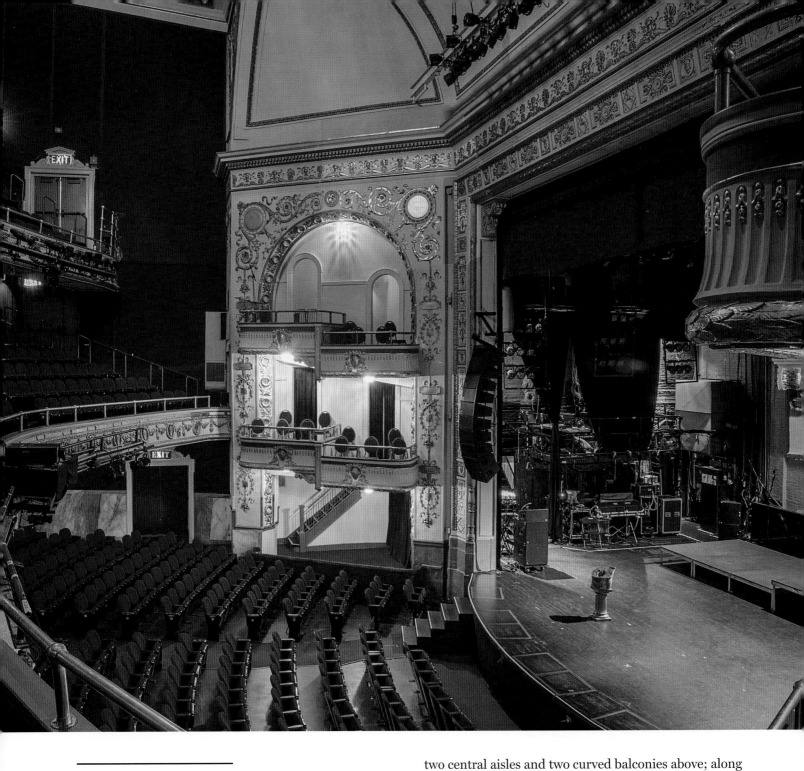

The balconies are sharply curved, providing good views of the stage. The gilded plasterwork decoration surrounding the boxes also covers the proscenium opening.

two central aisles and two curved balconies above; along with the Belasco (also designed by George Keister), the Apollo is among the few remaining theaters with two balconies. The neoclassical proscenium is flanked with monumental arches, while similar arches frame the double tiers of boxes, and a foliate-ornamented frieze and cornice wraps across the boxes and the stage. A cornice circles the coved ceiling, forming another monumental arch and a semicircular dome. Tall colonettes and plasterwork repeat classical motifs, as do the square columns that support the balconies.

By the 1970s, the Apollo had fallen on hard times as the popularity of live entertainment waned, the neighborhood deteriorated, and audiences dwindled. Used as a movie theater and for live performances without big stars, the Apollo faltered under changes of ownership and closed in 1979.

In 1981 politician-entrepreneur Percy Sutton led a group of investors to purchase the theater in a bankruptcy sale and revive it as an entertainment complex, recording studio, and television production center. The venture was unsuccessful, and in 1991 the Apollo was acquired by the state and a nonprofit foundation was established to operate it. Though it remained popular with tourists and continued its legendary Amateur Nights, it continued to struggle, unable to attract big-name black performers. In 2001, major restoration projects were begun on the exterior and interior with funds from state, city, and private sources. The distinctive facade was refreshed, and the interior was brought back to life under the direction of Beyer Blinder Belle Architects & Planners and Davis Brody Bond Architects and Planners, creating a harmonious dialogue between new elements and historic ones. The Apollo remains a work in progress but shines again in its transformed neighborhood as a place "where stars are born and legends are made."

From the stage, most of the decorative impact comes from color rather than ornament.

Grand Central Terminal

1913

One of the best-known and most-visited spaces in the city, the Main Concourse has natural light streaming in from three tall arched windows at the western end. Upper walls are subtly variegated Caen stone, while the lower portions are clad in rich-looking and more durable marble.

Overleaf: The barrel-vaulted ceiling features the celebrated mural by French artist Paul Cesar Helleu of the night sky with the constellations of the winter Zodiac. Many stars were illuminated to give a twinkling effect.

89 East 42nd Street, Manhattan
Reed & Stem, Warren & Wetmore
Interior designated 1980

More than 750,000 passengers use Grand Central Terminal every day, but most rush through without pausing to notice their surroundings. Those who do, however, experience what many consider the most spectacular public space in the city, and a world-renowned landmark. The Main Concourse, with its fifteen-story-high star-studded ceiling, grand staircases, immense chandeliers, and ornate metalwork, has been compared to majestic European cathedrals. A superb example of Beaux-Arts architecture, both inside and out, the terminal marks a milestone in the historic preservation movement, having been saved from development plans that would have destroyed the interiors and mounted a fifty-story tower atop its iconic facade. Refreshed by a major restoration in its ninth decade, Grand Central is now a modern commuter center with dining and retail facilities that make it a destination in itself.

In 1903 the New York Central Railroad began to plan for a new terminal to replace the outdated 1871 Grand Central Depot and its larger 1899 successor. Long-distance and commuter train travel had been made increasingly attractive by the electric trains that were replacing steam locomotives, which were banned by the State of New York after 1908. A competition was held to design the new facility, and Reed & Stem's design was chosen over that of such celebrated firms as McKim Mead & White and Daniel Burnham. The railroad, however, hired Warren & Wetmore to design the facade. The two firms finally, if somewhat reluctantly, collaborated on the project as associated architects. Some 150,000 people attended the inaugural ceremonies on February 2, 1913, and the design drew praise across the country and internationally. With forty-four platforms and sixty-seven tracks on two levels, it was the largest railroad station in the world.

Through the main entrance on 42nd Street or the Vanderbilt Avenue porte-cochère, visitors enter the marble-clad concourse, whose barrel vault is painted with the signs of the zodiac on a celestial ground. Conceived by Whitney Warren and French artist Paul César

TO VANDERBILT AVENUE
AND TAXIS

WEST BALCONY

WAITING ROOM   TRACKS 3

SHUTTLE PASSAGE

DINING CONCOURSE   TRACKS 110 TO 117

In a marble-clad passageway, massive chandeliers light the way down a ramp to the lower level.

The four-faced bronze clock that tops the circular information booth is a landmark meeting place for travelers.

Helleu, the 35,000-square-foot mural was executed by fifty artists, who lay on scaffolding to paint the 2,500 stars depicting a Mediterranean winter sky. (The image is reversed—it is thought that the artist wanted to show the sky as seen by God.) A four-faced clock of brass and opalescent glass is mounted on the information booth at the center of the space. This focal point is crowned with an acorn (the symbol adopted by the Vanderbilts, chief owners of the railroad, evoking the adage "Great oaks from little acorns grow.") Acorns and oak leaves, as well as foliage, serpents, and symbols of speed, commerce, and progress, are sculpted in stone and bronze ornamentation throughout the interior. Virtually every design element in the terminal's overscaled spaces is equally grand: the four-tiered, acorn-festooned bronze chandeliers in the Main Waiting Room weigh 2,500 pounds each. Marble staircases lead from the concourse to the mezzanine, and pedestrian ramps access the lower level, which houses the fabled Oyster Bar and the adjacent "whispering gallery." At either end of the hall are monumental lunette windows decorated with winged locomotive wheels and incorporating walkways across the vast space.

Grand Central was innovative in technology; the first terminal designed exclusively for electrified trains, it was illuminated by 4,000 individual light bulbs. Its centralized hot water heating system was the largest of its kind. And its vast underground structure, requiring the excavation of more than three million cubic yards of dirt and rock, created stacked tunnels beneath Park Avenue to accommodate a network of tracks and heavy equipment, as well as the weight of the building itself.

In the years before they were supplanted by automobiles and airplanes, trains were the primary means of long-distance travel, and Grand Central was an appropriately glamorous location from which to begin a journey. Its most famous train was the 20th Century Limited, a luxury New York Central train traveling to and from Chicago. After World War II, however, with the growth of the suburbs and new highway construction, the terminal became a commuter hub, and its use an everyday occurrence.

The station deteriorated, a victim of both the waning popularity of train travel and the assumption that old buildings, even grand civic structures, inevitably become obsolete. A 1945 restoration was insufficient to halt the decline. But the destruction of Pennsylvania Station in 1963 to make way for Madison Square Garden changed public attitudes toward preservation, dramatized the need for a landmarks law, and helped to catalyze the establishment of the Landmarks Preservation Commission in 1965. Two years later Grand Central Terminal became one of the city's first designated landmarks.

When owner Penn Central proposed to erect a Marcel Breuer–designed tower on top of the terminal (obliterating the interior), the Commission rejected the plan. Penn Central sued, and a court invalidated Grand Central's landmark status. The terminal remained imperiled until a group of dedicated preservationists, including Jacqueline Kennedy Onassis, brought national attention and political pressure to the campaign. In 1978 the United States Supreme Court upheld the landmarks law, saving the terminal and setting an important precedent reaffirming the authority of cities to preserve historic buildings.

Despite the designation of its interior two years later, Grand Central continued its decline, and by the last decade of the century had become a shadow

of its once-magnificent self, with a grime-encrusted ceiling and oversize billboards obscuring many of the architectural details. The turnaround began in 1990 when Metro-North, which had taken over the terminal for its commuter train service in 1982, undertook a ground-up restoration, allocating half of the budget to the interiors.

Led by Beyer Blinder Belle Architects & Planners, the project took ten years, reversing the decline of the building and the interiors, and adding practical amenities. Billboards, including a much-maligned Kodak Colorama sign, were removed, ramps reopened, and a new staircase on the east side of the concourse (mirroring the original one on the west side) was added to create a balcony observation deck and restaurant spaces.

Some changes have been technical: the departure display board, once slip panels, is now on LCD screens, and the light bulbs have been converted to fluorescents. The tasteful addition of shops and dining facilities has kept the splendor of the great space intact.

But the most visible—and most welcome—improvement is overhead: the constellations on the ceiling now sparkle as they did a century ago (one

Bronze and glass lighting fixtures in the Graybar passageway to Lexington Avenue.

Unexpected classical detail on the ceiling, looking from the ramp into the Main Concourse.

The marble-and-bronze ticket counters remain the same, though the signage above them has been modernized.

At the subway entrance, a section of Guastavino ceiling tile.

dark patch on the upper north corner remains to show the pre-cleaning difference).

The *New York Times* greeted the restoration as the "greatest feat of historical preservation in the city's history," and Grand Central Terminal today stands as one of the city's proudest monuments and major attractions.

Cunard Building

1921

The ceiling decoration, designed by Ezra Winter, incorporates coffers, rosettes, and arabesques, framed by cartouches with images of historic sailing vessels.

25 Broadway, Manhattan
Benjamin Wistar Morris, Carrère & Hastings
Interior designated 1995

The extravagantly colored vaulted-ceiling interior of the Cunard Building recalls the days when ocean liners were the chosen mode of transatlantic travel for the privileged few. Cunard Steamship Company was a leader in the luxury fleet that traveled between America and Europe in the years after World War I. The Great Hall interior set the scene for the clients arriving to purchase tickets for passage on the company's grand steamships.

The building itself, the first major structure erected in New York after the war, on the largest site in lower Manhattan, is a massive twenty-one-story structure with a distinctive H-shape silhouette and two "light-courts" that illuminate the spectacular ornamental effects in what is still one of the city's grandest spaces. The vestibule and the Great Hall are separated by iron grilles—the work of famed metalsmith Samuel Yellin. The hall itself is an octagon flanked by square arms, each broken up by

niches. The central dome and vaults on either side are enveloped in intricately detailed polychrome murals with images suggesting seafaring and the ocean: mythological figures, seals of English shipping towns, and exotic sea creatures. Pendentives below the dome bear images of the historic ocean-going vessels of Leif Ericsson, Christopher Columbus, John Cabot, and Sir Francis Drake, and maps of the continents by Barry Faulkner. In niches between the walls and vaults, stone reliefs depict the winds and the four seasons. With its walls of Roman travertine, the space evokes the grandeur of great Roman baths.

Nova Scotia businessman Samuel Cunard, co-owner of the first Canadian steamboat to cross the Atlantic, founded the Cunard Steamship Line in 1840. The company began as a carrier of mail and packages between Boston and England, expanding into passenger travel with the late-nineteenth-century wave of immigration to America. After World War I, Cunard began to focus on the luxury tourist trade, adding new ships and impressive headquarters buildings in New York and Liverpool.

As airplanes began to supplant ocean liners for transatlantic travel, extensive offices and elaborate ticketing facilities like those in the Great Hall became

The dumbbell shape of the building, a response to new zoning requirements for light and ventilation, created two "light courts" that admit natural light to the interior.

Iron gates by Samuel Yellin define a library-like area added inside the entry after the building was completed, with a carved stone fireplace, wood cabinetry, and a mural depicting a map of the world.

superfluous. Cunard reduced service and sold the New York building in 1968, moving its headquarters uptown. The Great Hall was vacated in 1971 and remained empty until the building was sold again and the new owner leased the space to the U.S. Postal Service. Handren Associates converted it to serve as a post office branch from 1977 until 2000, and the extraordinary ceiling decorations were covered over but unharmed. When the post office closed, the hall remained vacant and neglected for more than a decade, hidden from sight except for offices in the building with views into the "light courts." For a happy ending, the space was leased by Cipriani, restored, and inaugurated in fall 2004 as Cipriani 25 Broadway, where it now hosts receptions and special events, its decoration once more visible in all its splendor.

Fred F. French Building

1927

551 Fifth Avenue, Manhattan
Sloan & Robertson, H. Douglas Ives
Interior designated 1986

In the years following World War I, high-rise office buildings were changing the Manhattan skyline. Their proliferation reflected the thriving real estate market, and their distinctive setback silhouettes resulted from zoning regulations enacted in 1916.

The Fred F. French Building was designed at the height of this building boom, as the Art Deco style was beginning to flourish in America. Described by the Landmarks Preservation Commission as "among the finest commercial palaces of the late 1920s," it was the corporate headquarters for the leading real estate developer whose name it bears.

Fred Fillmore French began his career in 1908 and became known for his financial skills as well as his real estate expertise. Avoiding the usual practice of financing his building through banks, he raised funds through small investors. He also used in-house designers for most of his projects, which included the Tudor City residential complex. But for his flagship building, he wanted an eye-catching advertisement and an admirable work of architecture. He chose Sloan & Robertson, an established firm that would later design two important Art Deco skyscrapers in Midtown—the Chanin and Graybar Buildings. His chief in-house architect, H. Douglas Ives, was probably in charge of overseeing construction.

At thirty-eight stories, the brick-and-limestone structure was, when built, the tallest on Fifth Avenue. It is distinctive for its flat roof and stepped setbacks, but even more for the vivid polychrome faience panels on its facade, mixing Near Eastern motifs with symbols of commerce, progress, and integrity. Equally arresting is the massive bronze-framed main entrance on 45th Street, inspired by the ancient Ishtar Gate, suggesting New York's role as the new Babylon; the entrance on Fifth Avenue is similar but smaller.

Revolving doors lead into the L-shaped lobby, which continues the design theme of the exterior ornament; it is a striking marble-and-bronze space in a dazzling mix of styles, more exotic than Art Deco in feeling, alluding to both the ancient and the modern worlds. Despite its

Modern glass doors and a multi-paned gilt-bronze transom have replaced the original doors in the 45th Street entry.

relatively modest size, the interior makes a commanding design statement with golden-veined gray marble walls, a gilded-plaster frieze, and a spectacular painted ceiling—a marked contrast to the unadorned lobbies in most office buildings of the time. The ceiling is stenciled with blue-and-gold geometric patterns, mixing Near East and Egyptian motifs with Mayan, Viennese, and Moderne elements. The floors are beige Italian travertine with diamond-shaped Kato stone inlays and a black-and-white marble border. Eight bronze and crystal chandeliers, designed by the architect, are etched with numbers designating the elevator courts. Twenty-five gilt-bronze doors, some inset with panels symbolizing commerce and industry, complete the decorative scheme. Other attractions for potential tenants included technical advances such as an electrical plumbing system, easily controlled lighting and ventilation, and self-leveling elevators.

From its opening, shortly before the onset of the Depression, the building became a prestige address for Midtown offices, and its lobby has remained virtually unchanged except for the enclosure of the main entrance vestibule behind glass doors. In 1985 the French Building was purchased by Metropolitan Life, which undertook a major restoration that included repainting the ceiling and regilding the trim to restore the original patterns and palette of the lobby interiors. In 2002 the building was purchased again, and Li/Saltzman Architects undertook another restoration of the lobby walls and ceiling as well as the exterior envelope, helping to ensure its ongoing presence as an office building with a distinct personality.

Figures symbolizing Industry, Commerce, Finance, and Building are incorporated in the recessed panels of the gilt-bronze elevator doors.

The Fifth Avenue entrance features a different but complementary ceiling motif. The gray-gold marble walls are unadorned, except for the gilded frieze.

Williamsburgh Savings Bank

1929

At the apsidal end of the banking hall, Ravenna Mosaics created a bird's-eye view of Brooklyn with the bank at the center.

1 Hanson Place, Brooklyn
Halsey, McCormack & Helmer
Interior designated 1996

If the great banking hall of this building calls to mind a cathedral, that's precisely what its designers wanted. It was, in fact, a monument to finance and, in the words of the Landmarks Preservation Commission "the almost religious act of the savings bank depositor." The 512-foot-high tower with its four-faced clock was the tallest structure in Brooklyn when built, and it still dominates the skyline. Inside its massive doors, images suggesting industriousness and thrift are executed in luxurious materials and finishes for an interior that is both intriguing and individualistic.

The elaborateness of the Romanesque Revival banking floor belies its origin as a secondary location—the Williamsburgh's main building was in its namesake neighborhood, and branch banks were relatively new, permitted by state law only since 1923. The central location of this branch, in the Fort Greene area near shopping, entertainment, and local transportation, was chosen to serve as large a community as possible and to encourage its use by the growing number of women depositors, a fact made evident by the inclusion of a ladies' lounge.

The interior is set asymmetrically to the main entrance to maximize light from the long street frontage through the 40-foot-high windows. The marble-floored entry, its groin-vaulted ceiling a mosaic of gold stars on a blue sky, leads into a 63-foot-high basilica-like banking hall. On the far wall, in place of an altar, is an aerial view of Brooklyn in mosaic showing the Dutch colonial settlements and major city landmarks and placing the new Williamsburgh building at its axis, central to the borough it serves. The mosaic on the soaring ceiling, by the painter Angelo Magnanti, is a muted rendering of the mythological figures of the zodiac in a gold field. The intricately patterned marble floor of alternating round and square motifs, modeled on medieval Italian Cosmati work, is another striking feature of the exceptionally rich interior.

Emulating the custom of medieval church architecture, virtually all of the ornament has symbolic meaning. Carved figures on the marble columns represent industry,

Tellers stations occupied the arcades along either side of the space.

transportation, government, education, finance, and commerce, while sculptures on entrance gates and elevator doors depict occupations, from carpenter and plumber to engineer and lawyer. The sculptures are by Rene Chambellan, whose work adorns many of the city's notable Art Deco buildings. In contrast, enameled steel grillwork frames teller's windows and is also used for the chandeliers. In the center of the banking floor, glass-topped check-writing tables with fixed table lamps are virtual artworks in themselves, graceful notes in a space that blends fine materials with skilled craftsmanship.

Over the years, the bank was taken over first by Republic National Bank, and then merged into HSBC, and professional offices and commercial tenants occupied the office areas of the building. After the bank moved out, the building underwent a major redevelopment and restoration. The tower above was converted to luxury condominiums in 2006, and after briefly housing a local flea market, the grand banking floor and the vault below have been returned to public use as a special-events venue. Doorways have been changed and the check tables moved, but the key decorative elements remain, maintaining the essential character of the space.

Like the grillwork screens and the chandeliers, the glass-topped check-writing tables are gracefully detailed in bronzed metal.

A starry sky in mosaic covers the vaulted ceiling of the entrance vestibule.

Gold mosaics by Angelo Magnanti incorporate astronomical motifs and the mythological figures of the zodiac as well as the W monogram.

Film Center Building

1929

Kahn's use of color was as architectural as it was decorative; strong horizontals help to unify and visually expand the small space.

630 Ninth Avenue, Manhattan
Buchman & Kahn
Interior designated 1982

The building boom of the 1920s gave New York a new skyline and, less obviously, a new interior landscape of Art Deco lobbies. One of its finest and most colorful interpretations is the little-known interior of the Film Center Building, an office building west of the Times Square theater district, in the newly gentrified Hell's Kitchen (now Clinton) neighborhood.

In the late 1920s, a variety of firms involved in the young and thriving motion picture industry sought to locate their headquarters conveniently near the Times Square movie palaces. The Film Center Building was built to house the offices of film distributors, editing rooms, and related businesses. Reinforcing its association with current fashion, the building was decorated in the latest style, the American interpretation of the French-born Style Moderne, later renamed Art Deco. Design was not its only attraction: to accommodate the specialized clientele, every floor was equipped with steel vaults for storage of nitrate film. Although most of the original tenants have long since departed, the striking ground-floor spaces continue to attract tenants and to delight passersby as well as design aficionados.

In a relatively limited space, Ely Jacques Kahn, one of the most prominent architects working in the new style, ingeniously treated color as part of the structure rather than as decoration alone. The environment he created is strikingly theatrical, contrasting materials and textures with an interplay of light and shadow that eschewed the spare simplicity of the International Style, then in its early ascendance. The entry vestibule, featuring a geometric pattern of horizontal and vertical bands across the ceiling and down the walls, leads into a rectangular elevator lobby, where broad bands of alternating black and silver-gray stone run horizontally around the walls, visually expanding the relatively narrow space. As in the vestibule, molded plasterwork on the walls and ceiling defines horizontal and vertical elements in varying degrees of relief, creating the effect of a woven tapestry, and drawing the eye to the abstract pattern of the brightly colored mosaic on the far wall.

146

The ceiling is a gilded landscape of channeled grooves and ziggurat-like projections that frame the space. Cast-bronze elevator doors, vent grilles, staircase risers, and even the mailbox and directory board are adorned with varied abstract motifs, some suggesting stylized movie cameras. The ochre, pink, and gray terrazzo and marble floor is patterned in geometric shapes outlined by a black border.

The Film Center Building lobby has been carefully maintained, and it is a rare survivor of the film industry's early years; the building still houses many businesses involved in film, theater, music, and audio production and distribution

The elevator doors incorporate geometric patterns in relief, complementing the ceiling design.

The directional pattern on the floor leads to the elevator doors and draws attention to the brilliantly colored mural beyond them.

The asymmetry and animated effect of the mosaic play off of the precise patterns of the other surfaces.

Loew's Paradise Theater

1929

The studio of Caproni and Brother in Boston produced most of the sculptures in the theater, including plaster reproductions of works by Michelangelo.

2403 Grand Concourse, Bronx
John Eberson, Beatrice Lamb
Interior designated 2006

Loew's Paradise, completed on the eve of the Depression, was the showplace of the Bronx, an opulent escapist environment that could be enjoyed for as little as twenty-five cents. Though its golden years ended with the intrusion of television and the development of the multiplex, its flamboyant interiors are rare survivors, offering a glimpse into the years when going to the movies was a special event.

The Paradise was one of five "Wonder" theaters built for Loew's in the New York area—the others were the Valencia in Queens, King's in Brooklyn, the 175th Street Theater in Washington Heights, and Loew's Jersey in Jersey City. The company was founded in 1904 by Marcus Loew, who began his business with nickelodeons and transitioned into vaudeville and then into movie houses, creating the oldest theater chain in the country. By 1927 he owned 144 theaters. As the industry grew, so did the

theaters, which became increasingly larger and more elaborate, encouraged by the invention of sound and "talking pictures," and culminating in the grand movie palaces designed by specialists like John Eberson, Thomas Lamb, and Walter Ahlschlager.

Eberson, who designed the Paradise, originated the concept of the "atmospheric" theater, an alternative to movie palaces based on the Beaux-Arts European opera house. His idea was to evoke more romantic settings, drawing on Italian, Persian, Spanish, or Egyptian architectural precedents and adding ceilings that replicated a star-filled sky. He sought ambience rather than authenticity, creating exotic ornament from his imagination and fabricating most of it in his own workshops. Working with his wife, Beatrice Lamb, an interior decorator, and his son, Drew, he designed some 1,200 venues throughout several decades.

The 45,000-square-foot Paradise interiors are divided into several areas, each different but all equally ornate, in a flamboyant display of marble, mirrors, brass, and painted plaster. The theater is L-shaped in plan, with the auditorium perpendicular to a succession of progressively narrowing spaces: a recessed vestibule,

a low-ceilinged foyer, and the extravagantly decorated,
double-height grand lobby, overlooked by a promenade on the floor above. The wood-paneled walls and
doorways are outlined with gilded moldings. The floor
is marble, and the vaulted ceiling features elaborate
plasterwork and nine rococo-style murals by Andrew
Karoly and Lajos Szanto, framed in gilded-plaster
cartouches. The two-level auditorium, with a seating
capacity of almost 4,000, is wedge-shaped, narrowing
toward the stage. Plasterwork facades, twisted columns,
classical statuary, urns, caryatids, and archways wrap the
proscenium and continue along the walls, simulating the
courtyard of a grand palazzo. The outdoor ambience is
furthered by plaster birds and foliage and a star-dotted
deep blue ceiling, the latter an illusion that was adopted
in many theaters of this kind. The balcony is cantilevered

152

to avoid blocking views, and indirect lighting is concealed behind stained glass or recessed coves.

The original design included a machine that created artificial clouds, which traveled across the sky. Altogether, the auditorium was a tour de force of artifice and decoration; even lounges and washrooms had similarly lavish decor.

In the decades following World War II, many movie palaces closed; some were converted to other uses, and others were demolished. The Paradise suffered from waning audiences and the decline of the neighborhood around it. In 1973 it was divided into two theaters, and in the 1980s into a quadruplex, with dividing walls installed in the auditorium. But business continued to decline, and the badly deteriorated theater closed in 1994. Fearing that the interior would be gutted and the statuary sold, community leaders petitioned for landmark status, which was granted with a unanimous vote, but only for the exterior. The Landmarks Preservation Commission declined even to hold a public hearing on the designation of the interior, believing that it had already been too severely altered. The interiors were further damaged by a fire in 1996, just as preservationists were working with the owner on an adaptive reuse strategy, leaving a planned restoration incomplete.

A new owner rescued the building. Once EverGreene Architectural Arts restored the interiors, Loew's Paradise reopened as an entertainment venue in 2005. Seven months later, the Landmarks Preservation Commission finally designated the interior, citing it as "one of the most amazing spaces in New York City," though the *New York Times* called it "an architectural acid trip." In 2012 the Paradise was reincarnated once more, this time as the World Changers' Church, and in its new role it again attracts crowds and accolades.

The wood-paneled grand lobby features decorative ironwork and ceiling murals by painters Andrew Karoly and Lajos Szanto. A grand staircase leads to the promenade and upper foyer.

Beacon Theater

1929

The splendor of the auditorium comes largely from the rich colors, but the Oriental ambiance derives from faux-drapery that suggests a desert tent.

2124 Broadway, Manahattan
Walter W. Ahlschlager, Rambusch Decorating Company, Rapp & Rapp
Interior designated 1979

The only one of the original Manhattan movie palaces still in use as an entertainment venue, the Beacon was commissioned in 1926 as the Roxy Midway—a precursor of Radio City Music Hall, to be managed by impresario Samuel "Roxy" Rothafel as a venue for movies and live-entertainment spectacles. The original architect, Chicago-based Walter W. Ahlschlager, worked in a variety of styles, and designed hotels and office buildings as well as the 1927 Roxy Theater (demolished in 1960). For the Beacon project, he collaborated with the Rambusch firm, but when the original developer went bankrupt, Warner Brothers took over and hired Rapp & Rapp to complete the building. The theater finally opened in 1929 as Warner's Beacon, as a showcase for the newest trend in entertainment—talking pictures. Its name was taken from the beacon on top of the hotel in which it was housed; the combination of hotel and theater was a new building type.

The 2,600-seat, three-level theater is an exuberant profusion of styles, from classical to rococo to lavish orientalist. The low-ceilinged, semicircular outer lobby, featuring a gilded ticket booth, opens into a marble-walled, Renaissance-style inner lobby that leads in turn to the rotunda grand foyer—each successive space providing a new and exciting experience. The foyer design was based on that of the original Roxy, with a coffered ceiling and a thirty-foot-tall Venetian-style chandelier. Sculptural plasterwork encircles the space with colonnades, pilasters, and an ornate frieze above a mythical landscape painted by Valdemar Kjoldgaard. A hallway leads to the climactic three-level auditorium, an exotic oriental fantasy that gave the theater the nickname "Baghdad on Broadway." The deeply coffered ceiling simulates a tent, with plaster faux drapery in intricate multicolor Moorish-style patterns, echoed in similar effects on loge and balcony fronts. The proscenium is flanked by fluted columns and statues of Greek women warriors on pedestals. Across the top, a plaster drapery is faux-embroidered with a great gilded sunburst, and above the urn-topped

gilded arches on the side exits, Kjoldgaard painted large murals of Middle Eastern galleons and traders. Hundreds of elaborate fixtures highlight the gilding and sculptural ornament that embellish every surface.

The Beacon functioned as a first-run movie theater until 1974, when it became a live-entertainment venue for popular attractions like the Grateful Dead. It was subjected to sporadic and misguided renovations, but unlike many other movie palaces, it never closed. In 1986 the Landmarks Preservation Commission approved plans to repurpose the Beacon interior as a disco and restaurant. A "Save the Beacon" committee petitioned, and ultimately sued. After an intense, five-year campaign waged by hundreds of volunteers, entertainers, and philanthropist Brooke Astor, the Beacon was rescued and returned to its role as a music and entertainment hall.

In 2008 Madison Square Garden Entertainment, a division of Cablevision Systems Corporation, began a renovation and restoration of the theater. Beyer Blinder Belle Architects & Planners, working with EverGreene Architectural Arts, researched archival photos and architectural plans to restore the original decor, using elements of both Ahlschlager and Rapp & Rapp's designs. By that time, most of the ornament had been obscured beneath multiple coats of paint, much of the

In the Grand Foyer, a thirty-foot-tall Venetian-style chandelier hangs from the coffered ceiling. Over the gilded doors, a mythical landscape by Valdemar Kjoldgaard is framed by an elaborate frieze.

plasterwork was missing, the foyer wainscoting was covered with mirrors, water leaks had damaged the ceilings, and the original seats and carpet had been replaced. The rotunda's chandelier had not been operational for years.

Murals were repaired and restored; a Rambusch mural in the grand foyer, designed but never installed, was re-created and put in place; seats and carpeting were reproduced from archival photos; and lighting was rewired and modernized, making discreet use of LED technology to restore the original illumination effects. Less visible, but equally important, the mechanical systems were upgraded, and a state-of-the-art sound system was installed to enable the reborn Beacon to function as a multipurpose venue for modern performing arts, with its extraordinary interiors revived.

The auditorium ceiling is intricately patterned with Moorish motifs, as is the elaborately draped proscenium.

Mark Hellinger Theater

1929

Literally crowning the proscenium curtain is a sculpted baroque crown like those on royal bedsteads. Above it are cartouches framing rococo fantasy scenes.

237 West 51st Street, Manhattan
Thomas Lamb; Rambusch Decorating Company
Interior designated 1987

The last of the 1920s movie palaces built in the Times Square area, the Mark Hellinger was noteworthy for its ornamental profusion. Its interiors are a showpiece of baroque/rococo exuberance, a fantasy surround of plasterwork, painting, and gilding that rivaled the on-screen performances and now provide a background for an entirely different kind of observance.

Originally named the Hollywood Theater, the Mark Hellinger was built for Warner Brothers, the first to introduce "talking pictures," by one of the most prominent theater designers of the time. Thomas Lamb designed three hundred movie theaters and many for live productions all over the world. Named for the center of the new film industry, the Hollywood was designed as a movie house with stage facilities to present the live vaudeville shows that accompanied the films.

Warner Brothers was founded in 1904 by four siblings, pioneers in the filmmaking business (Rin Tin Tin was their first major star) and competitors of such major movie studios as Paramount, MGM, and First National. The growth of the business led to the development of a new type of venue, the specialty movie palaces that offered affordable, escapist entertainment in the decades of economic depression and war. Their spectacular interiors were part of the movie-going experience; the theaters were aptly called "palaces for the people." The Mark Hellinger is one of the most palatial and, with a capacity of some 1,500, among the largest.

The oval grand foyer (originally accessed through an entrance on Broadway, which was closed in 1936) is larger and more elaborate than those in other theaters of its kind. Eight two-story-high fluted Corinthian columns surround the space and support a domed ceiling decorated with a mural of nymphs and clouds, with an ornate bronze chandelier suspended from the center. Curved balconies project from between the columns, and a grand staircase like those in European opera houses leads to the mezzanine. Fabric-covered walls are framed

The grandeur of the space is enhanced by its curved configuration and by the high-relief plasterwork integrated into every surface.

The double-height grand foyer, one of the most elaborate in the Times Square area, is encircled by grand Corinthian columns. An ornate chandelier is suspended from a romantic ceiling mural.

A staircase curves up from the foyer to the mezzanine balcony.

with decorative molding. Lamb worked with Rambusch Decorating Company and its chief designer, Leif Neandross, on the decor, which includes carved and gilded ornament evoking rococo and neoclassical styles.

The auditorium, also oval in shape, is even more elaborate than the grand foyer. The domed ceiling, with another extravagant bronze-and-glass chandelier, is painted in a delicate Adamesque style, while the twelve murals in gilded-plaster cartouches encircling the ceiling evoke the French rococo. Virtually every surface in the theater is painted, gilded, or covered with exuberant high-relief plasterwork of baroque scrolls, shells, friezes, and cherub heads.

Just four years after opening, the Hollywood began presenting theatrical productions, alternating between showing movies and staging plays until 1949, when Warner Brothers sold it. Under new ownership, it was renovated into a "legitimate" theater and renamed for the Broadway columnist and former Warner Brothers producer Mark Hellinger. Like many of its neighbors, the theater struggled through the decline of the Times Square area. After the demolition of the Morosco and

the Helen Hayes in 1982, the Mark Hellinger was among more than forty theaters considered for designation by the Landmarks Preservation Commission at public hearings beginning in 1985. Two years later, it was, along with the Belasco, in the first group to be designated (both interior and exterior).

In 1989 the Mark Hellinger was reincarnated as the Times Square Church, a rare example (along with the Loew's Paradise Theater) of a landmark-designated interior used for religious purposes, made possible only because designation predated the change of function. Its interiors have been carefully maintained in their original condition, and the church now draws capacity crowds to the venue that once hosted *Casablanca*, *My Fair Lady*, and *Jesus Christ Superstar*.

In the main lobby, the elaborate plasterwork includes swags, scrolls, cherubs, and cartouches, all richly gilded.

Cartouches with painted panels inspired by eighteenth-century French imagery are inserted in the cove below the ceiling.

Chrysler Building

1930

405 Lexington Avenue, Manhattan
William Van Alen
Interior designated 1978

The Chrysler building epitomizes American Art Deco style. Designed at the height of the 1920s skyscraper-building boom, it is one of the most striking examples of this short-lived but highly influential style, and its ground-floor interior is a vibrant, energetic space that evokes movement and modernity. Few remember that this interior was once threatened by a 1970s "modernization" effort soon after it was designated a landmark. Fortunately, the Landmarks Preservation Commission held firm, and the Chrysler interior escaped the worst of the proposed changes, and remains its unique and individualistic self.

The architect William Van Alen had been retained to design a 60-story office building on a busy corner near Grand Central Station when Walter Chrysler acquired development rights to the project in 1928. Chrysler was aggressively expanding his automobile company and

his own interests, and the building was to become a corporate symbol as well as a personal one, although it was paid for out of Chrysler's own pocket. He asked Van Alen to design a building taller than the Eiffel Tower: at 1,046 feet and 77 stories, it became the world's tallest, edging out 40 Wall Street with the last-minute addition of a 185-foot spire. Though it was surpassed in height by the Empire State building within a year, it is still the world's tallest brick building, and with its spire and exterior ornamentation, an instantly recognizable silhouette on the New York skyline.

As iconic as the exterior has become, the interior is equally distinctive: a flamboyant space that matches its exuberance and originality. Three separate entrance lobbies, one at each corner, lead to the triangular main concourse, an expanse of red Moroccan marble interrupted by two massive octagonal piers that channel traffic to the elevator corridors. The floor, of yellow Siena travertine, is set in a diagonal pattern that is not only decorative but also functional, serving as another directional device. In contrast, entry and service doors, decorative railings on the marble staircases to the mezzanine and lower level, and framing on shop windows and directories are all

of polished steel; the metalwork is an allusion to automobile trim.

On the ceiling a mural by Edward Trumbull is organized into three thematic sections: one symbolic of primitive energy, another evoking the construction of the building, and a third tracing the development of modern transportation, particularly airplanes, all joined by Machine Age motifs that relate to the patterns on walls and floor. Over the main entrance is an image of the building itself. Lighting is provided by lamps enclosed in steel troughs on vertical panels of polished onyx, arranged in a stepped pattern. Light reflecting off the panels casts a warm glow.

The most arresting decorative elements in the lobby are the twenty-eight elevators, arrayed in four marble-lined corridors. These are ornamented with an abstract lotus pattern inlaid in metal and exotic

Angled ceilings draw the eye to the Edward Trumbull mural that spans the space. The three-section mural follows the triangular form of the interior, and includes references to transportation and the construction of the building.

wood veneers. The elevator interiors are also decorated in abstract patterns of inlaid wood, some suggesting Egyptian influence; each bank of elevators has a different design.

The idiosyncratic decor of the Chrysler Building, with its unbridled display of sunbursts, ziggurats, gargoyles, and sculptures suggesting radiator caps was not an immediate critical success. Van Alen's extravagant ornament was derided as superficial kitsch, particularly by admirers of the International Style, then coming into fashion, which eschewed both ornament and symbolism. But the general public was captivated, and when interest in Art Deco was revived decades later, critics recognized the building's importance as an archetype of the style and of the skyscraper form.

The Chrysler family sold the building in 1947, and ownership subsequently changed several times. As the neighborhood declined and occupancy plummeted, the interior was neglected and mistreated. In the 1970s the Massachusetts Mutual Life Insurance Company bought the building in foreclosure. The Landmarks Preservation Commission had not yet focused on the city's Art Deco skyscrapers, but it moved to designate the Chrysler Building shortly after designating Radio City Music Hall in 1978. The owners protested interference with its renovation efforts, which included extensive changes to the lobby, the most drastic of which was a proposed elaboration of the elevators. Resisted by the LPC, the plan was finally dropped, and the building was sold.

New owners have taken a more conservative approach. In 1999 EverGreene Architectural Arts restored the ceiling mural, which had been coated in polyurethane that had darkened over time, making it almost impossible to see. Despite the presence of security turnstiles—a precautionary feature installed in many office buildings after 9/11—the lobby interior retains its dynamism and its continuing appeal.

The dramatic lighting fixtures are panels of Mexican onyx, staggered vertically in front of the elevator corridors and street entrances and fronted by vertical steel reflector troughs fitted with lamps. Light reflects off the panels to create warm, glowing illumination throughout the space.

Empire State Building

1931

The 34th Street corridor, reserved for tenants and their visitors, features a marble reception desk with a stainless-steel top. On the balcony level a new fixture is suspended from the bold tray ceiling.

350 Fifth Avenue, Manhattan
Shreve, Lamb & Harmon
Interior designated 1981

Welcoming the millions of tourists who visit New York's—and perhaps the country's—most popular landmark every year, the ground-floor areas of the Empire State Building are as iconic as its celebrated exterior. Designated an interior landmark despite unfortunate modernization in the 1960s, it has, thanks to a sensitive restoration completed in 2011, been returned to its former glory.

Described in the official designation report as "overwhelming," the soaring marble lobby is indeed that: a cathedral-like space, half a city block long, with its most arresting features a two-story relief of the building exterior, rendered in polished aluminum, and a spectacular aluminum and gold leaf celestial ceiling mural. Two-story corridors along the elevator core create grand concourses on either side, intersected overhead by aluminum and glass bridges. Throughout the space,

bold geometric ornament evokes the machine aesthetic that characterized "skyscraper style," designations later incorporated into the Art Deco style.

Not the first to bear the name, an homage to New York State's nickname, the Empire State was successor to a nine-story office building at 640 Broadway and was built on the site of the original Waldorf-Astoria Hotel at the then-extraordinary cost of $52 million. A competitor in the frenzy of skyscraper construction just before the Depression—the stock market crashed two weeks after the project was announced—it was completed in a record 410 days. It was planned and promoted as the world's tallest building, at 1,248 feet surpassing both the recently built Chrysler Building and 40 Wall Street. Topping off its 102 stories, a slim spire and mast were intended as a docking site for dirigibles; deemed hazardous, it was never put to use.

The building's progress was enthusiastically followed by the media and by business and political figures. Former New York Governor Alfred E. Smith laid the cornerstone, and President Herbert Hoover pressed a button in Washington, D.C., to turn on the lights when the building opened on May 1, 1931. New York

Governor Franklin D. Roosevelt was one of hundreds of special guests attending the daylong celebration, and when the public was admitted the following day, thousands streamed in to visit the observatory and admire the interiors.

The Empire State was hailed as "a milestone marking the beginning of modernism" and widely admired for its understated elegance—the work of chief architect William Lamb—eschewing the flamboyant decor that marked many buildings of the time, including the Chrysler Building.

The recent restoration of the lobby to its original design was part of a major upgrading of the building, completed in 2011 by Beyer Blinder Belle Architects & Planners. Guided by historic documents and photographs, original blueprints and drawings, the designers

Tourists entering from Fifth Avenue are greeted by a relief panel depicting the building. The ceiling is a meticulous reproduction of the original in aluminum and gold leaf, designed by Leif Neandross.

The anemometer over the information desk, installed to measure wind speed at the top of the building, where dirigibles would dock.

Medallions inset in the walls honor the various trades that worked on the construction of the building.

worked with Jones Lang LaSalle, Rambusch Decorating Company, and EverGreene Architectural Arts to restore, replace, or re-create elements that had been deteriorated or covered up. Damaged sections of the book-matched marble were replaced, surfaces were cleaned and polished, and twelve thousand feet of artisanal cast-glass fixture lenses replaced acrylic inlays that had been installed in the 1960s "modernization." Chandeliers designed to be hung over the second-floor pedestrian bridges but never made were fabricated from the original drawings. The most impressive accomplishment was the re-creation, by more than fifty artisans, of the original aluminum- and gold-leaf Leif Neandross ceiling mural, which had been painted over and covered with an acrylic dropped ceiling. Paying tribute to the Machine Age, the mural uses industrial gears and wheels to suggest stars and planets in a celestial panorama. State-of-the-art lighting now re-creates the original illumination of the lobby, highlighting the mural and enabling current and future generations of visitors to experience the space as its designers always intended.

Radio City Music Hall

1932

1260 Avenue of the Americas, Manhattan
Associated Architects, Edward Durell Stone
Donald Deskey, interior designer
Interior designated 1978

The interiors of Radio City Music Hall are as much an attraction to visitors as the performances presented in them. An innovative translation of the traditional movie palace into a modern vocabulary, it was the first completed project in Rockefeller Center, and a part of the complex called Radio City, after its prime tenant, Radio Corporation of America (RCA). The world's largest indoor theater, Radio City featured an innovative interior design that included a radical new seating configuration and technical advances beyond anything previously seen. Equally noteworthy was the integration of major artworks all based on the theme "The Progress of Man." It was, and remains, as the Landmarks Preservation Commission designation report commented, "one of the most impressive achievements in theater design in the country."

In 1978, however, this extraordinary work of theater design was threatened with demolition. In an unusually bold move, the LPC, using its relatively new and untested power to protect interiors, moved swiftly to designate Radio City's grand foyer, auditorium, staircases, mezzanines, and even bathrooms and lounges—by far the largest interior designation in New York City. This early victory for the preservation of interiors came almost simultaneously with the United States Supreme Court's decision upholding the designation of Grand Central Terminal.

Like all aspects of Rockefeller Center, the music hall was a team effort. Edward Durell Stone, who later designed the Museum of Modern Art's first building, was chief of design, reporting to Wallace K. Harrison. The interiors were masterminded by Donald Deskey, who became one of the pioneers of the industrial design profession but was relatively unknown when he won the competition for the music hall. His plan avoided "palaces for the people" extravagance, favoring modernistic rather than Beaux-Arts style. He designed more than thirty separate spaces for the theater, including eight men's and women's lounges, or smoking rooms, that are distinctive for their sophisticated use of new materials like Bakelite

The dramatic black-and-gold entrance lobby is low-ceilinged, a prelude to the open space beyond.

In the grand foyer, the strong vertical lines of the glass chandeliers are repeated in wall sconces on the mirrored side wall. Ezra Winter's monumental mural *The Fountain of Youth* is based on an Indian legend referring to the ambitions of life.

Overleaf: Still the largest interior auditorium of its kind, the oval space is column-free and shallow, with good views from every seat. The curved plaster ceiling is formed of eight overlapping arches that repeat the form of the proscenium.

and aluminum, along with classic marble, crystal, and gold foil. In addition to the interiors, Deskey designed furniture, carpets, wall coverings, and lighting fixtures, and chose the artists whose work would be displayed.

As was the case in many theaters, the interiors were planned as a series of escalating experiences, from the relatively dark, low-ceilinged ticket lobby to the grand foyer and finally the auditorium. While the early twentieth century movie palaces were generally amalgams of contrasting styles, Radio City is consistent in design, using scale, color, and variety of pattern to differentiate the spaces.

The ticket lobby, in black and red with black terrazzo floors and brass trim, opens into the three-story-high, elliptical grand foyer, with a gold ceiling, two tall glass

chandeliers, and matching crystal wall sconces. A broad, curving staircase leads to its focal point, the immense *Fountain of Youth* mural by Ezra Winter. Fifty-foot-tall gilded mirror panels on one wall reflect the guests and add a festive note. The color scheme of warm, dark tones carries through to the carpet, which has a pattern of abstract musical instruments by noted textile designer Ruth Reeves.

Entry into the auditorium is through eleven pairs of steel doors with bronze reliefs by sculptor Rene Chambellan, whose work is seen on the exteriors of the American Radiator, Chanin, and Daily News Buildings in New York. The auditorium itself is a sweeping oval space, reaching eighty feet in height, and entirely free of columns; the design was influenced by Josef Urban's

On the lower level, a dramatic mood
is created with black walls, mirror-
faced piers and diamond-shaped
light fixtures.

1929 landmark auditorium for the New School for Social
Research. Three shallow mezzanines, rather than one
deep balcony, create a more intimate connection with the
stage and allow good views from any of the 6,200 seats.
Above the huge proscenium, a series of eight concentric,
overlapping arches create the effect of a giant sunburst.
The great gold curtain, the world's largest, conceals
technology that includes a revolving stage turntable,
hydraulic lifts for special effects, a movable orchestra pit,
and equipment to produce rain, fountains, or fog. The
complex lighting system, concealed in coves between the
arches, was controlled by a board in front of the stage,
emitting different colors in harmony with the music of an
RCA-developed Wurlitzer organ, the largest ever made.

Down a flight of stairs from the lobby, the lounge
level is a darkened space with black walls, deep blue
carpet, and murals by Louis Bouché. The lounges were
given as much attention as the theater proper. Artwork

for men's and women's facilities on each floor was com-
missioned from such notable artists as sculptor William
Zorach, ceramist Henry Varnum Poor, and painters
Stuart Davis, Witold Gordon, and Edward Buk Ulreich.

Implementing the vision of celebrated impresario
Samuel L. "Roxy" Rothafel, Radio City Music Hall
opened on December 27, 1932, with an elaborate variety
show, but within two weeks converted to a movie-and-
stage-show format that drew thousands of visitors
to Rockefeller Center. Business declined in the postwar
years, when audiences began defecting to television,
suburbia, and the multiplex. Although the Christmas
show and the Rockettes remained successful, the music
hall was not profitable as a live-entertainment venue.

In 1978 Rockefeller Center announced plans to close
the theater and build an office tower over the building,
triggering public protests and demands for the Landmarks Preservation Commission to save the interiors,
which were considered more important than the exterior.
A public hearing attracted more than a hundred speakers
and included a kick line of Rockettes, who danced on the
steps of City Hall. Some questioned the LPC's authority
to designate a commercial interior—the only precedent

was the Gage & Tollner restaurant in Brooklyn, which had owner support. Over Rockefeller Center's objections, the LPC designated the music hall's interiors, the first part of Rockefeller Center to be protected. The owner sued, but let the case drop after the state Urban Development Corporation funded renovations and imposed a new management structure that proved the historic theater could turn a profit. It reopened in 1980 after extensive renovations.

The most recent and by far the most comprehensive restoration came in 1999, when the music hall closed for seven months to undergo a complete rehabilitation by Hardy Holzman Pfeiffer Associates and the Rockwell Group, reversing interim changes that had diluted the original design. The interiors were returned to their original color schemes; fabrics and wall coverings were re-created from archival photographs and samples; and the theater reopened in October 1999.

Radio City Music Hall now operates year-round, presenting a variety of programs, including pop concerts, music awards, and live stage shows, as well as the annual Christmas show featuring the iconic Rockettes, which continues to enchant a new generation of youngsters and their families.

Fanciful leaf-patterned fabric by Margaret Mergentine covers the walls of a powder room.

A men's smoking room features a "Maps of the World" mural by Witold Gordon, and leather-covered furniture by Donald Deskey.

Stuart Davis painted the bold mural in the downstairs smoking lounge.

Theatrical scenes in bronze bas-reliefs by Rene Chambellan decorate the double stainless steel doors leading to the auditorium.

AT&T Long Distance Building

1914, 1916, 1932

32 Avenue of the Americas, Manhattan
McKenzie, Voorhees & Gmelin; Voorhees, Gmelin & Walker
Interior designated 1991

This interior is housed in what was the world's largest long-distance communications center, the last of several major skyscrapers built in AT&T's years of greatest expansion. The fashionable Art Deco scheme of the ground-floor spaces was equally notable for its iconography, highlighting the importance of national and international communication in a technologically advancing world.

After Alexander Graham Bell's mid-1870s invention, the telephone business generated many small regional firms, which eventually merged into the American Bell Telephone Company. Its subsidiary, the New York–based American Telephone & Telegraph Company (AT&T), was incorporated in 1885 to handle long-distance traffic connecting the regional companies. It quickly became the heart of the Bell System, and its purpose-built skyscraper reflects that importance.

The original seventeen-story structure was built in 1914 as the Walker Lispenard Building, named for two of the bordering streets, and was shared by AT&T and Western Union. Seven floors were added two years later as AT&T continued to expand, and the irregular-shaped structure was enlarged once more in 1932 to reach its present configuration, twenty-eight stories high and spanning most of a city block. Cyrus Eidlitz (son of Leopold, one of the architects of the Tweed Courthouse) was lead architect of the original structure, and the successor firms designed the expansions. The final renovation reflects the preferred style of Ralph Walker, a leading proponent of Art Deco. Walker, who had previously worked for York & Sawyer, had also designed the Barclay-Vesey and Western Union Buildings (both interior landmarks), using a similar decorative approach.

"Modernistic," as Art Deco was then called, was America's mix of French Style Moderne with images of the Machine Age. Its abstracted forms and flat patterns were perfect complements to the linearity of the setback skyscrapers. The elaborate iconography of the Long Distance Building's first-floor interior proclaimed AT&T's commitment to international communication and a

modern aesthetic. Decorative motifs include symbols of the telephone and radio and their reach to the farthest corners of the world, as well as elements suggesting weaving, which may refer to "weavers of speech," as long-distance operators were called.

Inside the high-ceilinged Sixth Avenue entrance is a striking mosaic map of the world, and the ceiling is decorated with allegorical figures of four continents, linked by golden telephone lines. Both were the work of Hildreth Meière, the most prominent muralist of the day, who

worked on projects in St. Bartholomew's Church, Temple Emanu-El, and the exterior of Radio City Music Hall.

The lobby extends the length of the building on a somewhat irregular path. Varying ceiling heights divide the space into sections, which are unified by a band of

A mosaic map of the world in the Sixth Avenue entrance suggests the power of communication to connect nations.

colored glass mosaic that runs along walls and ceiling. Other unifying decorative features are the burnt orange marble baseboard and pilasters of Indian red tiles. The terrazzo floor is off-white with gray borders and gray stripes to guide circulation.

Benefiting from continuing ownership by the same company, the interiors have undergone only minor changes: two elevator openings were blocked and signage was added, as were benches, planters, ashtrays, and security panels, but at the time of designation in 1991, the design of the lobby remained intact. In 2001 Fox & Fowle completed a renovation that added new infrastructure and restored the lobby to Walker's original design. Today the building is a modern communications hub that embraces the history that made it possible.

Allegorical figures along the ceiling represent continents: a female figure and kangaroo for Australia, a reclining figure, tiger, and pagoda for Asia, and an Egyptian queen and the pyramids for Africa.

RCA Building

1933

Immediately inside the entrance are two murals by Jose Luis Sert, *Time* on the ceiling and *American Progress* behind the information desk.

30 Rockefeller Plaza, Manhattan
Associated Architects
Interior designated 1985

Originally named the RCA Building, this was the first and is still the most important structure designed for Rockefeller Center, the largest privately financed architectural project in the country and a visionary example of successful urban planning. The complex bears the name of its founder, John D. Rockefeller Jr. Although many neighbors were speculative buildings, 30 Rockefeller Plaza was designed for a specific tenant, General Electric's Radio Corporation of America (RCA) and its subsidiary National Broadcasting Company (NBC), pioneers in the expanding industry of radio and television. The importance of RCA to Rockefeller Center is suggested by the name Radio City, which was often applied to the entire complex.

Like the rest of the group, 30 Rockefeller Plaza is credited to a collaboration of three architectural firms. And like all of the buildings, it was planned to incorporate significant artworks—in this case, a series of murals that are the lobby's principal ornament and one of its major attractions. The sophisticated treatment of the space, and the choice of materials and colors, set the tone that would be maintained throughout Rockefeller Center.

In the latter part of the 1920s, Rockefeller, who had funded several architectural restorations and donated the land for the Museum of Modern Art, began acquiring properties in what was then a disreputable neighborhood in Midtown, for a cultural center to be anchored by a new Metropolitan Opera House. That plan proved impractical, and the project became a commercial development, on land leased from Columbia University. Ground was broken in 1931 and construction of the complex continued until 1939, through the Great Depression. Though it met with criticism and at first struggled to find tenants, Rockefeller Center became a prestigious and profitable office, retail, and entertainment complex, and its buildings—30 Rockefeller Plaza in particular—are now considered among the period's most successful designs.

The seventy-story structure terminates the east-west axis, with its main entrance facing the Plaza. With two million square feet of rentable space, it was for years the

Brass strips outline concentric squares on the dark marble floors, acting as both ornament and directionals.

Handsome bronze railings grace the stairways leading to the lower-level concourse and up to the mezzanine.

Square bronze planters hold seasonal flowers.

world's largest office building in floor area. The ground floor and mezzanine were designed as a unit, following the linear forms of the exterior, with a decorative scheme in tones of ivory and dark gray marble inlaid with bronze accents. The two-story entrance lobby, a relatively narrow space, connects to shop-lined concourses that flank the central elevator banks. Massive square, bronze-inlaid marble columns punctuate the space, helping to direct traffic. On either side of the lobby and in the center of the building, curving marble staircases access the mezzanine balconies and an underground concourse.

Immediately inside the entrance, a dark gray marble reception desk stands in front of a mural by José María Sert entitled *American Progress*. Light fixtures on the marble piers illuminate his mural, *Time*, on the ceiling. Sert, Diego Rivera, and Frank Brangwyn were originally commissioned to paint themed murals on the lobby walls: Rivera's to illustrate a vision of a better future, Sert's to express man's mastery of the universe, and Brangwyn's to honor man's relation to society and his fellow man. Rivera's work was covered over and then removed after the artist refused to delete a prominent image of Lenin. Other murals wrap around the elevator halls, depicting various symbols of communication, in recognition of the building's original tenants.

Floors throughout are black terrazzo with gray-green inserts and inlaid bronze strips forming concentric squares. Bronze grilles, moldings, and shop-window trim, alabaster light fixtures, and exotic wood–lined

elevator cabs complete the decorative scheme, maintaining the consistency of modernist decor.

As with the other buildings in the Rockefeller Center complex, 30 Rockefeller Plaza was not an immediate success, and at first struggled to find tenants. But along with its neighbors, it became part of a prestigious and profitable office, retail, and entertainment complex, and is considered among the most significant designs of its era. Although the name—and the billboard-height logo at the top of the building—has changed, from the RCA Building to the GE Building in 1988, and to the Comcast Building in 2014, it has been in continuous use since its completion. The landmark spaces remain prime examples of the streamlined modernistic style, though the years took their toll on the murals, until a major restoration in 2009 removed layers of yellowed varnish and returned them to their original brilliance. At the heart of Rockefeller Center, 30 Rockefeller Plaza is today one of the city's most visited landmarks, the home of major television shows and the glamorous Rainbow Room, and it provides a backdrop for the celebrated Christmas tree.

Rainbow Room

1934

The Rainbow Room is most romantic at dusk as the city lights begin to sparkle.

30 Rockefeller Plaza, Manhattan
Associated Architects
Elena Bachman Schmidt, interior designer
Designated 2012

To countless New Yorkers, mention of the Rainbow Room evokes fond memories of family celebrations, social events, or romantic dinners and dancing. Its skyscraper-top location and theatrical scale made it one of the city's most glamorous venues and a rare Art Deco space that architect Robert A. M. Stern called "a tour de force of the Modern Classical style" and the *New York Times* labeled "the most cinematically perfect space in New York."

The Rainbow Room came into being as a supper club on the sixty-fifth floor of the seventy-story RCA Building. Originally envisioned as public space, the top six stories had been built with terraces and a two-story space especially suited for a dining room. The idea of private clubs or restaurants at the tops of skyscrapers (like the Cloud Club in the Chrysler Building) was in

vogue, and Frank R. Darling, hired in 1933 to manage restaurants and observation roofs at Rockefeller Center, was assigned to develop the project. Darling had worked for amusement parks and fairs, and he developed the floor plans of the observation decks, bars, game rooms, and the Rainbow Room. The name was inspired by the color organ that RCA-Victor had developed in the 1920s and installed at Radio City Music Hall, which converted music into colored lights. In the Rainbow Room, concealed lights illuminated the dome and dance floor, changing hues according to the mood of the music.

Wallace K. Harrison's design for the Rainbow Room drew inspiration from Josef Urban's designs for nightclubs like the Central Park Casino (1929) and the Persian Room at the Plaza (1934), though the idea of a revolving dance floor dated to Murray's Roman Gardens on 42nd Street, which opened in 1915 and closed during Prohibition.

Construction of the Rainbow Room began shortly after the repeal of Prohibition, and its design was a relief from both dim-lit speakeasies and the somber Depression. Designed in the latest and most fashionable modernistic style, it was a light-filled space; a stream-lined composition of curvilinear forms, enhanced by

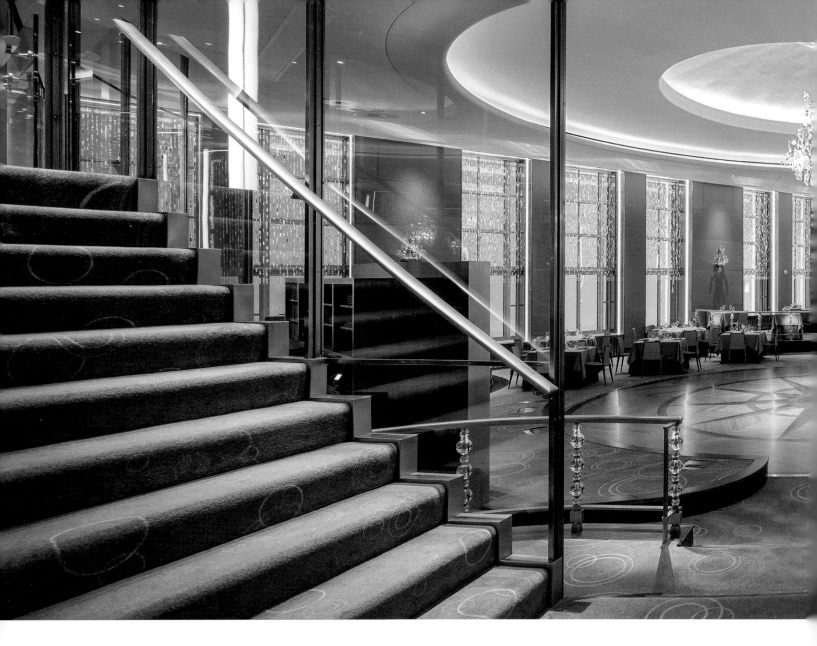

The circular dance floor and shallow backlit
dome, part of the original design, were
reinterpreted for a contemporary look.

warm colors, rich materials, and flattering illumination.
Interior designer Elena Bachman Schmidt, who had
worked with Elsie de Wolfe before establishing her own
firm, was responsible for color schemes, materials, and
finishes, and Vincent Minnelli, who designed sets for
Radio City Music Hall and later became a celebrated film
director, worked with her on color and lighting.

Getting to the Rainbow Room was something of a
special occasion in itself: a private bank of high-speed
elevators (one of which, at 1,400 feet per minute, was the
fastest yet on record) whisked visitors up from ground
level to the sixty-fifth floor, where a short hallway opened
onto the double-height, column-free space framed by
twenty-four oversize windows that were the defining
element of the room, wrapping around the space almost
from floor to ceiling. Sweeping city views created an
illusion of floating in the sky, with rooftops and stars providing both decoration and a stunning view.

Guests entered from a corner of the room, down two
sets of broad steps to a circular dance floor. Thirty-two-
feet in diameter, it could revolve in either direction every
three or five minutes. Around the dance floor, three
tiered levels held table seating for about three hundred
diners. Over the dance floor, a dome concealed recessed
lighting, and a brass-canopied crystal chandelier hung
from its center. Mirrors were important elements, as
was lighting in crystal chandeliers and sconces draped in
prisms, stars, and balls. Colors were intense but understated: aubergine walls and draperies, and deep green

carpet patterned with a Greek key motif. The orchestra space was at one side of the dance floor, and a balcony above served as an elevated stage for entertainers. Opposite were mirrored faux columns that concealed spots and floodlights; most other lighting was indirect. Adjoining the Rainbow Room was the Patio, renamed the Rainbow Grill the following year. Attire for dinner, which cost $3.50 per person, was formal except on Sundays.

The Rainbow Room became a popular location for parties, charity benefits, and galas, drawing half a million people to such events in its first four years of operation, and the Rockefeller Center Luncheon Club functioned as a private facility, mostly for tenants of the center's office buildings.

Despite its popularity, consistent profitability proved elusive. The Rainbow Room closed in December 1942, though it continued to operate as a luncheon club, and

reopened in 1950 as a cocktail lounge. A succession of owners initiated renovations, most of which retained the original design. It closed in 1962 to be refurbished with plum silk walls, mirrored columns, and gold satin draperies. In 1975 live music and dancing were reintroduced.

The Rainbow Room closed again in January 1986 for a Hardy Holzman Pfeiffer renovation that returned it more or less to the original design through painstaking archival research, including the re-creation of the original compass rose pattern of the dance floor. Alterations included a new entrance, a glass wall behind the entertainers' balcony, and a new computer-controlled lighting system.

The restored space, operated by celebrated restaurateur Joe Baum, opened in December 1987, but lasted only eleven years before closing again. Still another tenant redesigned it as a private party venue, but departed after lease disputes with Tishman Speyer, who had purchased the fourteen-building Rockefeller Center complex in 2000. In January 2009, the Rainbow Room and luncheon club closed, leaving the space vacant for three years.

Although the Rainbow Room had been earlier proposed for interior designation, the LPC hesitated, uncertain whether enough of the original design remained. It was finally designated in 2012, with the approval of the Rockefeller Center owners. Gabellini Sheppard Associates undertook a restoration that would reimagine the interior to accommodate contemporary needs while burnishing the room's historic past. The Rainbow Room reopened in 2014 with a refined color palette of grays and pewter, a white-gold-leaf ceiling, a newly reconstructed dance floor reprising the original compass rose motif, and glittering strands of crystal veiling the windows. It remains a special-occasion venue, tinged with a remembrance of glamorous times past and primed for new memories to be made.

The new interpretation of the Rainbow Room introduces shimmering crystals at the windows and crystal balusters supporting brass railings.

American Museum of Natural History Theodore Roosevelt Rotunda

1936

Central Park West at 79th Street, Manhattan
John Russell Pope
Interior designated 1975

Commanding the main entrance to the American Museum of Natural History, one of the largest institutions of its kind in the world, the Theodore Roosevelt Rotunda is both an introduction to the museum and a commemoration of the life of a New York governor and the country's twenty-sixth president. Formerly called Memorial Hall, the space includes striking murals depicting his achievements, but the memorial elements compete for attention with the world's most dramatic dinosaur fossil display in the center of the hall: a rearing forty-five-foot high Barosaurus facing an attacking Allosaurus.

The museum, founded in 1869 (one of the founders was Theodore Roosevelt Sr.), was first housed in the Arsenal in Central Park, moving to its own building in 1877. That Gothic Revival structure by Vaux & Mould is now surrounded by subsequent additions. In 1908 Cady, Berg & See designed the Romanesque structure that faces 77th Street. Beginning in 1922, Trowbridge & Livingston added several wings and the Hayden Planetarium. An impressive entrance on Central Park was the next step, and the idea was floated for New York State to use the opportunity to honor former President Theodore Roosevelt, who had been an accomplished explorer and naturalist as well as a politician. A competition was held for the design of a New York State memorial commensurate with his stature. Pope's gray granite Memorial Building, enclosing the rotunda, was the winning entry.

The grand triumphal arch of Memorial Hall's Beaux-Arts exterior leads into a monumental space, more than one hundred feet long and one hundred feet high, with natural light streaming in through large arched windows at either end. The walls are faced with marble wainscoting and limestone above, and quotations from Roosevelt's writings are etched into the limestone beneath the entablature. The floor is of geometrically patterned marble. Three murals by William Andrew Mackay appear in recesses on either side of the hall and opposite the entrance, marked by pairs of red marble Corinthian columns. The paintings recall events in Roosevelt's life: his African expedition, the Treaty

of Portsmouth, and the digging of the Panama Canal. Mackay was used to working on a large scale; he had been a pioneer of painted camouflage for ships during World War I.

The Memorial Building was considered a significant building, as a symbol both of America's prestige and of Theodore Roosevelt's importance to its history. Governor Franklin Delano Roosevelt laid the cornerstone in 1931 and, as president, was the featured speaker at the opening ceremony five years later.

The American Museum of Natural History has continued to grow. It now consists of twenty-five interconnected buildings with forty-five exhibit areas. The Theodore Roosevelt Rotunda remains one of its most noteworthy spaces. Its restoration, completed in 2012, was the first phase of a master plan prepared by Kevin Roche John Dinkeloo and Associates. The vivid murals, newly polished marble, and the imposing dinosaurs ensure that the space will continue to provide visitors with a grand introduction to the museum.

Sunset Play Center
Bath House

1936

Seventh Avenue at 43rd Street, Brooklyn
Herbert Magoon
Interior designated 2007

This colorful interior is the entrance to one of eleven large outdoor pools built in a single summer, in every borough of the city, as part of a program to build recreation centers in underserved neighborhoods. They were financed in a unique city-federal government partnership under the Works Progress Administration (WPA). The brainchild of Mayor Fiorello La Guardia's parks commissioner Robert Moses, the pool complexes could accommodate 49,000 users simultaneously. All but one are still in use for their original purpose.

The Depression had intensified the need for recreational spaces, particularly in crowded city neighborhoods, and this type of project suited the objectives of President Franklin Delano Roosevelt's New Deal programs, which promised relief, recovery, and reform to the country. One of those programs, the Works Progress Administration (WPA) created jobs for the unemployed

by funding major public-works projects, such as those initiated by Moses in his various positions in city and state government. Called the "Master Builder," he was responsible for bridges, tunnels, expressways, and parks that changed the landscape of the city, and Mayor La Guardia secured much of the financing for those ambitious plans.

Although the design of the Sunset Play Center complex was a team effort, and Joseph L. Hautman, chief architect for the Parks Department, prepared plans and construction drawings, the bath house was designed by Herbert Magoon, the architect who had designed the Jones Beach bath houses. Magoon also designed the bath house in Crotona Park, in the Bronx, which opened a few days after the one at Sunset Play Center. In all of the facilities, the stipulation of low-cost materials in federal regulations suggested the use of cast concrete and brick, which were compatible with decorative schemes in the modernistic style.

The Sunset pool complex is located at the eastern end of Sunset Park, which had been developed at the turn of the twentieth century. The bath house forms its entrance and the hub of the complex; in designing

Magoon used modest materials
with imagination, creating an
appealing modernistic space that
updated a classical rotunda form.

it, Magoon made creative use of the modest materials
at his disposal to update a classical form with a modern
aesthetic. An entrance foyer leads into the lobby,
a domed rotunda with curving walls of brick laid in
Flemish bond below and smooth off-white plaster
above. Doorways set into the brick lead in and out of
the locker rooms. At the base of the clerestory level,
a row of cast-stone diamonds sets off the diaper-
patterned brickwork above, which is punctuated near
the ceiling by sixteen square windows. A massive
octagonal brick column, concealing lighting and
electrical cables, occupies the center of the space,
encircled by the colorfully tiled octagonal ticket
booth. The geometric-patterned floor is laid in stone,
glazed brick, and terra-cotta and blue tiles.

By the 1970s, many of the pool complexes were badly
deteriorated, reflecting both their heavy use and the
financial crisis then facing the Parks Department. The
city allocated funds to restore the Sunset Play Center,
and it reopened on August 8, 1984, with colorful murals
painted by local schoolchildren. The complex continues
to serve its neighborhood as a community gathering
place, an archetype of the WPA projects, and, according
to the Landmarks Preservation Commission, "among
the most remarkable public recreational facilities ever
constructed in the United States."

Marine Air Terminal

1940

A marble bust of former Mayor Fiorello La Guardia sits in the center of the main terminal space.

La Guardia Airport, Queens
Delano & Aldrich
Interior designated 1980

Celebrating the glamorous early days of transatlantic air travel, the main room of the Marine Air Terminal was a spectacular introduction to the adventure of flying and remains one of the city's most distinctive Art Deco interiors. The striking circular space is planned with rational simplicity: two stories high with a three-tiered, skylit ceiling. Deep green marble walls set off its defining feature: a vividly colored wraparound mural by James Brooks depicting the history of flight and man's quest to conquer the skies.

The gateway to the world's first transatlantic passenger flights, the terminal was inaugurated slightly more than a decade after Charles Lindbergh's legendary 1927 trip from New York to Paris. It was an original part of La Guardia Airport, at the time the world's largest and most expensive—built at the then-enormous cost of $40 million. Constructed on a site bordering Flushing Bay that once held an amusement park and later a private airfield, it was the city's first municipal airport. The project was a joint venture between New York and the Works Progress Administration (WPA), a New Deal organization that provided jobs by funding public-works projects. The airport was authorized by President Franklin D. Roosevelt and enthusiastically supported by Mayor Fiorello La Guardia, for whom it was named after it opened.

More than 325,000 people flocked to the airport's first day on October 15, 1939, not long after the opening of the New York World's Fair, just a mile-and-a-half away. The Marine Air Terminal was inaugurated several months later, on March 31, 1940, when a Pan Am Boeing 314, nicknamed the Yankee Clipper, made its first transatlantic flight. Carrying nine passengers, a ten-person crew, and more than five thousand pounds of mail, the plane landed in Lisbon eighteen and one-half hours later. The Clippers were seaplanes, able to land on water as well as land, and therefore considered safer than conventional aircraft for flying long distances over the ocean. With cruising speeds of 200 miles per hour, the elegantly appointed aircraft could carry seventy-four

passengers. They were hailed as faster but equally luxurious alternatives to the ocean liners that until then had been the only means of transoceanic travel. Their golden age ended when the planes were pressed into service in World War II; by war's end, new technology made them obsolete and the terminal was turned over to conventional aircraft.

In the ensuing years, the terminal suffered misguided efforts at modernization, including the painting over of the mural, which was mistakenly thought to contain Communist propaganda, in 1952. The first preservation efforts were led by aviation historian Geoffrey Arend, who helped raise funds to uncover the mural, which was restored by the artist and rededicated in 1980. Arend also initiated the move to have the building protected as a landmark, inside and out.

Visitors to the terminal today can see *Flight* restored to its original vivid colors. Painted on a linen ground in a style that reflects the Socialist Realism of the 1930s, it depicts both mythical and historic figures related to flying, from Icarus, Daedalus, Leonardo da Vinci, and the Wright Brothers to pilots, navigators, and passengers. The last mural done under WPA auspices, it was also the largest. Stainless steel, a new material when the terminal was built, bands the mural and appears on the doors leading out of the circular space, as well as on the propeller-blade motifs inlaid into the end panels of the waiting-room benches.

The 2004 restoration of the terminal by the Port Authority NY/NJ, overseen by Beyer Blinder Belle Architects & Planners and completed just in time for the sixty-fifth anniversary of its inauguration, included repairs to the exterior—most notably the reconstruction of an exterior frieze of flying fish—as well as the refurbishment of the interior, including cleaning the mural to reveal its original vivid hues.

The Marine Air Terminal is now the only active airport terminal in the country dating to the first generation of air travel. It services shuttle flights to Boston, Chicago, and Washington—a modest but vivid reminder of the days when flying was a novel and glamorous experience.

Above green marble walls, the wraparound mural by James Brooks commemorates aspects of man's explorations in flight: Icarus, astronomy, and modern aircraft.

Manufacturers Trust Company Building

1954

At the top of the escalator is the Harry Bertoia metal screen, reinstalled in the reconfigured interior. Escalators were originally installed parallel to Fifth Avenue.

510 Fifth Avenue, Manhattan
Skidmore, Owings & Merrill
Eleanor H. LeMaire, interior designer
Interior designated 2011

The Fifth Avenue building erected for the Manufacturers Trust Company was one of the most innovative and admired structures of its time. Its conversion from minimalist banking hall into two separate retail stores is a striking but controversial adaptation of an interior landmark to another use, which involved altering the orientation of the interiors.

The Landmarks Preservation Commission began considering postwar modernism with the 1980s designations of Lever House and the Seagram Building. By the mid-1990s, much of New York's midcentury heritage had become eligible for landmark status, but was also increasingly vulnerable to deterioration or remodeling. The Manufacturers Trust Company Building was designated in 1997, but only for its exterior—a surprising decision in view of its transparent facade and seamlessly integrated interior.

When it opened in 1954, the building was described as "unlike any other financial institution in this country or abroad." Instead of the customary classical structure, thought to connote stability and security, Gordon Bunshaft of Skidmore, Owings & Merrill (SOM) designed a luminous steel-and-glass cube. The glass facade famously showcased the massive steel vault, a message to depositors that its transactions would be open but its holdings secure.

Manufacturers Trust had pioneered many new services, leading to rapid growth and the need for larger facilities. Although the bank had acquired a corner lot on the southwest corner of 43rd Street and Fifth Avenue, the transfer of air-rights for an adjacent building limited the height of a new structure to a maximum of sixty-eight feet. Initially the bank retained Walker & Gillette, but plans for a classical limestone structure and then a multi-story glass one were delayed by building restrictions during the Korean War. By the time the restrictions were lifted, Walker & Poor (successor to the original firm) had been discharged and, the modernist movement having taken hold, the bank sought designers more suited to the new style.

The mandate for the new facility was that it must accommodate a high volume of customers, have an inviting ambience, and—an unusual requirement—be convertible to another use. SOM was given the assignment, and they conceived a building that marked a new direction in bank design. Chief designer Gordon Bunshaft was the chief designer, working with Charles Evans Hughes III (who conceived the idea of making the vault visible from the street), Patricia W. Swan, and Roy O. Allen; the decoration was assigned to prominent interior designer Eleanor H. Le Maire

The Manufacturers Trust building was designed as four stories plus a recessed penthouse and roof garden. Client services were on the ground floor and a cantilevered mezzanine supported on almost-invisible white marble columns, creating the illusion of a floating floor and leaving the glass facade undisturbed. Banking operations were visible from the street through a grid of glass panels framed in projecting mullions of polished aluminum. The panels are nine-by-nine feet at street level, larger on the second; at twelve by twenty-two feet, they were said to be the largest ever made in this country.

Anchoring the facade, the immense seven-foot-diameter thirty-ton steel vault, designed by industrial designer Henry Dreyfuss in collaboration with Mosler Safe Company engineers, was a decorative tour-de-force. The other prominent design feature was a pair of steel escalators, with unusual illuminated side panels designed by Le Maire, accessing the mezzanine. Set parallel to Fifth Avenue, they created a free-floating

diagonal to relieve the linearity of the design. The luminous ceilings of thin vinyl sheeting, a rare surviving example, were lit until 1:00 am, turning the interior into street-front window display.

Furnishings and ornament were minimal: free-standing desks, white-topped ebony counters, one wall of polished black granite and another painted blue, and slim rectangular flower boxes on both levels facing the street. Softening the austerity of the space, a screen of 800 enameled-steel plates by Harry Bertoia stood at the west end of the mezzanine, and a Bertoia wire sculpture was suspended over the escalators.

The bank opened on October 5, 1954, attracting 15,000 admiring visitors. It became a popular venue for photographers and fashion advertisements, and public tours in the first two years drew almost 10,000 people.

In 1961 Manufacturers Trust (whose name dated back to 1858) became Manufacturers Hanover Trust. By the time of its purchase by Chemical Bank in 1991, there had been several alterations to the building: the second level was converted to offices, automated teller machines blocked the view of the escalators, and the ceilings were changed. Further alterations in 1976 divided the ground floor in two, filled in the cantilever and installed partitions on the banking floor. Twenty

The vault is now a backdrop for fashion mannequins.

Detail of the vault.

years later Chemical bought Chase Manhattan, and in 2002 merged with JP Morgan to become JPMorgan Chase. In 2010, the bank vacated the building, removing the Bertoia screen and sculpture.

Though the space was intended to be adaptable to other uses, the new owners, Vornado Realty Trust, found the transparency and original configuration inconvenient to retain. When the Landmarks Preservation Commission designated the interior in 2011, Vornado secured approval to reconfigure the interior into two rentable spaces and commissioned SOM to retrofit their original design. The most extreme changes included reorienting the escalators to face new entrances on the Fifth Avenue facade. Preservationists took LPC and Vornado to court and won a settlement that returned the Bertoia pieces in 2012 on indefinite loan from Chase.

The conversion raises challenging questions about protecting modern interiors whose design is not executed on the walls, but within them, and where changes like moving doorways or escalators transform the very nature of the space. The remodeled Manufacturers Hanover interiors are well designed and aesthetically pleasing, but have little resemblance to the landmark original.

The reconfigured space, with two Fifth Avenue entrances and the rotated escalators.

The iconic Ezra Stoller view of the original building at night. The diagonal of the escalator counterbalances the verticality of the metal-framed windows.

Seagram Building

1958

Pristine as an abstract composition, the bronze reception desk and corridor doors are set off against terrazzo floors and travertine marble walls. Installed in squares, the marble has a subtle pattern.

---

375 Park Avenue, Manhattan
Ludwig Mies van der Rohe, with Philip Johnson
Kahn & Jacobs, associate architects
Interior designated 1989

New York's only design by Mies van der Rohe, the Seagram Building is an instantly recognizable glass-walled icon, boldly set back on a plaza facing Park Avenue. As in the Manufacturers Trust Company building, the lobby and exterior are inseparable, but in this case both received landmark designation at the same time—a recognition sought by the owners as soon as the building became eligible. It was the second modern landmark to receive designation (the first was Lever House), and, along with the Four Seasons Restaurant, the first modern interior landmark as well.

German-born Ludwig Mies van der Rohe, the last director of the Bauhaus, immigrated to the United States in 1937 and became a citizen in 1944. He had been designing office buildings since the 1920s and was celebrated for innovative glass-walled structures.

Samuel Bronfman, president of Joseph Seagram & Sons, sought an architect to design an appropriate building. He initially hired the firm of Pereira & Luckman, but his daughter, Phyllis Lambert, an architecture student, rejected their design and persuaded her father to consider Mies van der Rohe, who was more likely to create a significant work that would be a symbol of corporate achievement. She also suggested hiring Philip Johnson as Mies's associate on the project.

At the time, Park Avenue between 50th and 59th Streets was in transition from an exclusively residential stretch to a prestigious business location, and it offered an ideal venue for a work of architecture that would be treated almost as a work of art. The architects set the building back from the street, extravagantly using only 40 percent of the allowable space, and essentially positioning the design on a pedestal. At a cost of $41 million, it was at the time the world's most expensive skyscraper.

The lobby is entered through revolving glass doors. Interior and exterior are perceived as one contiguous space, integrated by transparent walls and a marquee over the entrance that is basically an extension of the lobby ceiling. The lobby is articulated in three conjoined

208

The severity of the space is modulated by the sophisticated lighting scheme and the warmth of bronze in architectural elements and trim.

The interior is a composition of horizontal and vertical planes, executed in rich materials for an effect that is at once spare and luxurious.

volumes: a rectangular front section, three elevator corridors in the center, and a T-shaped rear section. The walls and floors are travertine, and the ceiling is gray-glass mosaic set into black cement. Taking the place of ornament are elegant materials and finishes, precisely detailed. The custom-designed elevator cabs have polished bronze doors and interiors of steel and bronze mesh. They are lit by a grid of translucent white panels, part of a then-innovative illumination plan that included recessed fixtures and a luminous ceiling that casts a glow over the entire space. Bronze hardware and appointments echo the projecting mullions on the glass facade. Even signage was custom designed.

The project was a collaborative effort: Mies designed the building with the assistance of Philip Johnson; Kahn & Jacobs prepared the working drawings, and consultants included lighting designer Richard Kelly and graphic designer Elaine Lustig, as well as engineers, acoustical experts, and landscape architects.

Seagram moved into its offices on the first seven floors in December 1957. The plaza immediately became a popular public amenity in a bustling business location, and the building won countless accolades for its elegant

modern style. It became a prototype for modern corporate structures by Mies and countless others, most of whose interpretations fell far short of the original.

The company was so proud of its building that it applied for landmark designation when the structure was only twenty years old, which would have required a change in the landmarks law. When Seagram sold the building in 1980, remaining a major tenant, the company insisted on incorporating into their contract the stipulation that the new owners pursue landmark status as soon as the building became eligible, as well as guidelines for maintenance and upkeep, in order to protect its integrity.

Under still another owner, the Seagram lobby remains pristine and meticulously maintained. The LPC designation report noted that it was praised as "one of the best spaces built in Manhattan this century." And it is unlikely that the comment will become outdated.

The lobby entrance to the Four Seasons restaurant, up travertine steps and through bronze-framed glass doors. The Picasso curtain, "Les Tricornes," is now on display at the New-York Historical Society.

Interior flows into exterior, with the lobby ceiling continuing outward to form a marquee over the entrance from the plaza.

Four Seasons Restaurant

1959

The marble-framed pool, as conceived by interior designer William Pahlmann, remains a constant through the seasonal changes of foliage and table linens. Mies van der Rohe chairs and custom tableware complete the setting.

99 East 52nd Street, Manhattan
Philip Johnson
William Pahlman, interior designer
Interior designated 1989

The Four Seasons is one of the finest International Style interiors in the country. Located in what is certainly the iconic structure of the genre, the Seagram Building, it is as celebrated for its aesthetic as it is for its "power lunch" clientele.

Having commissioned a major work of architecture to burnish its public image, the Seagram Company wanted a fine restaurant to occupy a prominent space off the new building's lobby. On the recommendation of Mies van der Rohe, Philip Johnson, who had collaborated with Mies on the building and the lobby, was hired to design it. For the Four Seasons, Johnson recruited the celebrated interior designer William Pahlmann and lighting designer Richard Kelly. Pahlmann had designed the Forum of the Twelve Caesars for Restaurant Asso-

ciates, the firm selected to operate the new facility, and Kelly had been responsible for the illumination of the Seagram Building lobby.

The unusual configuration of the restaurant was determined by the architecture. The space is on two levels: on the upper level, the two main dining sections are separated by a corridor that opens off the Seagram Building's lobby; on the lower level, the main restaurant entrance, on the side of the building, opens into a foyer with travertine walls and floor. A broad, open travertine staircase angles up to the main level, where a shimmering Richard Lippold sculpture of slim, gold-dipped brass rods is suspended over the leather-wrapped bar, set off by subtle concealed lighting. The adjacent Grill Room has a clubby feeling, with walnut-paneled walls and plush upholstered booths. Light is filtered into the space through double-height windows covered with anodized-aluminum chains in tones of brass, bronze, and copper. Designed by textile artist Marie Nichols and hung like Austrian shades, the chains ripple gently in the air rising from the ventilation grills beneath, an effect not anticipated by the designers.

A study in contrast: the thin bronze railings of the angular stairway from the 52nd Street entrance, and the gentle swags of the anodized-aluminum chain curtains.

Richard Lippold's hanging sculpture of slim brass rods is a counterpoint to the massive form of the wood-wrapped bar.

The corridor provides a transition between the clubbiness of the Grill Room and the serenity of the Pool Room. A light-filled space with double-height ceilings, its centerpiece is a twenty-foot-square pool of white Carrara marble. The inspired idea of William Pahlmann, the pool provides an element of contrast in the expansive, table-filled space. At each corner, cylindrical bronze planters hold trees that are changed with the season, and small planters are suspended in front of the two windowed walls, which are fitted with the same aluminum chains as those in the Grill Room. The ceiling is a grid of off-white, perforated aluminum panels; the grid motif is echoed in the custom-woven carpet. Sleek furniture by Mies van der Rohe, Charles Eames, and Eero Saarinen, and custom glassware, silver holloware, and silver services by industrial designer Garth Huxtable and his wife, Ada Louise (later the influential architectural critic), complete the scheme of understated elegance. Following Edgar Bronfman's directive, all artworks installed in the space were modern: two Lippold sculptures, a Jackson Pollock painting, and a theater curtain by Pablo Picasso in the corridor (on loan from Seagram). In keeping with the International Style aesthetic, there is no additional ornament; the rich materials, textures, and lighting suffice. At a cost of $4.5 million, part of which was assumed by Seagram, the Four Seasons was at the time the most expensive restaurant ever built.

Restaurant Associates, founded in 1947, operated the original La Fonda del Sol and Brasserie. The firm's specialist, Joe Baum, is credited with the unique concept of the Four Seasons as a place in which the decor and the menu would change every three months in correlation with the seasons. It was an instant success. Food critic Craig Claiborne called it "the most exciting restaurant to open in New York within the last two decades." His praise was as much for the design as for the menu.

Minor changes were made to the interiors in the next several decades: a glass partition replaced the trellis of climbing ivy that separated the bar from the Grill Room dining area, a service desk was installed near the lobby entrance, and artist James Rosenquist painted a permanent mural for the mezzanine. A series of works had initially been commissioned from Mark Rothko, who completed the murals but reneged on the deal, considering the setting inappropriate.

The Four Seasons was purchased from Restaurant Associates by the chef and general manager, who requested landmark designation for the interior when the Seagram Building itself was being considered, in part to ensure the continuation of their business. The building's owner, while required by its lease with Seagram to seek designation for the exterior and lobby, opposed designation for the restaurant and sued when it became an interior landmark. The designation was upheld, and the Four Seasons became the second landmark restaurant (the Oyster Bar was designated in 1980, but as part of the Grand Central Terminal interior). The first landmark restaurant was Gage & Tollner, designated in 1975, which was recently covered over in a retail conversion. The Four Seasons has been more fortunate. Until his death in 2005, Philip Johnson oversaw sensitive updates to the interior, and in 2008 Belmont Freeman Architects was commissioned by the current owners, the Bronfman

family and restaurateurs Julian Niccolini and Alex von Bidder, to develop a long-term restoration master plan. In May 2015, the Seagram building owner presented plans for alterations to the restaurant interiors, which were rejected by the LPC.

An artwork in the restaurant generated controversy in 2014, when the current building owner proposed to remove the Picasso curtain (not owned by the restaurant and not included in the landmark designation), echoing the uproar when the Seagram collection of artworks by Miró, Rothko, and other modern masters was auctioned off in the early 2000s. The Picasso was given by the New York Landmarks Conservancy to the New-York Historical Society, where it is currently exhibited.

The rods of the Lippold sculpture sway, along with the chain curtains, with the movement of air from the ventilating system.

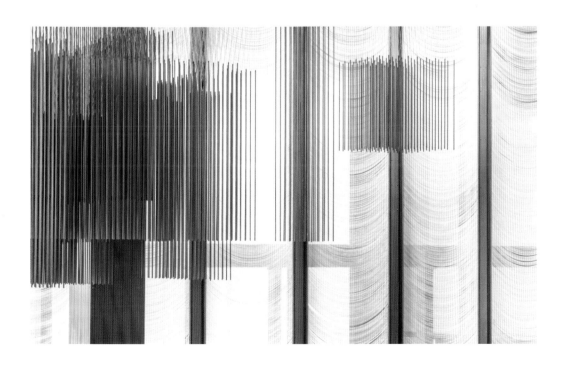

Trans World Airlines Flight Center

1962

The swooping curves of the interior create a feeling of movement, and were a unique achievement in an era long before computer-generated design.

John F. Kennedy Airport, Queens
Eero Saarinen & Associates
Interior designated 1994

With its sweeping, winglike silhouette and brilliant white exterior, the TWA terminal has been the symbol of flight for all arriving at Idlewild (now JFK) airport from the moment it was completed. It remains one of the most extraordinary structures of its kind. Its interiors are equally and possibly even more exceptional, one of the few iterations of organic modernism in a period when the starkly rectilinear International Style predominated. It is considered Eero Saarinen's masterpiece.

Within the soaring concrete structure, the interior is a series of interconnected curvilinear enclosures that create a walk-in sculpture, perhaps reflecting Saarinen's study as a sculptor before entering the architecture program at Yale. Like its exterior, which suggests a bird in flight, the dynamic space is almost entirely white, covered in half-inch circular ceramic tiles, with contrasts of tone and shadow lending variation to the monochromatic

surround. The vaulted central section is divided into three levels, with curving staircases accessing the main level and balcony, and tunnel-like walkways to the elevated satellite gates. Sculpted piers and archways opening off the side wings of the lobby create interconnecting passageways. The interior conveys a feeling of movement that "interpret[s] the sensation of flying," according to the Landmarks Preservation Commission. The consistency of organic form in every element, including signage, railings, counters, and furnishings, creates seamless transitions from one area to the next. Broad crescent-shaped windows offer views of aircraft movements, and narrow skylights connect the terminal passageways, with indirect lighting adding understated illumination. Suiting the modernist aesthetic, there is no ornament—the interior is its own decoration, except for bright red carpeting, seating, and signage in TWA colors.

When the Port of New York Authority (as it was then known) assumed responsibility for New York City airports in 1947, it began to plan an expansion of Idlewild to accommodate the explosive growth in air travel after World War II. Separate terminals for each airline began to replace the centralized terminal

Vivid red, keyed to the TWA logo, wraps the sunken seating in color and comfort.

A view of the runways, allowing passengers to monitor departures and landings from an enclosure that suggests a living-room environment.

scheme, reducing congestion and minimizing walking distances for passengers.

In the early 1950s, Trans World Airlines sought to compete with rival Pan American by introducing tourist-class transatlantic flights, switching to jet aircraft for transatlantic flights, and building a new terminal in New York. Saarinen's visionary and costly futuristic design was the result. Its up-to-the-minute features included more efficient ticketing and baggage-claim systems, electronically controlled doors, flight-information boards, and closed-circuit television monitors. The new concept of jetways—elevated, enclosed ramps leading from the gate right into the plane—were a last-minute addition that gave passengers easy, protected access to aircraft. The terminal opened on May 28, 1962, a year after Saarinen's death. The design was not without its critics, but its efficient operation and crowd-pleasing architecture soon

made it an iconic image of both jet travel and modern architecture. By the time the interior received landmark designation, a number of changes had been made, including the removal of the red carpeting and elements of signage, but the biomorphic form remained intact.

In the early 1990s, as the terminal became eligible for landmark status, the Port Authority advanced renovation and expansion plans for the structure to accommodate increased passenger traffic and larger planes. The LPC nevertheless moved to designate the terminal inside and out, accepting the challenge of dealing with changes to a working transportation hub while preserving its architectural integrity.

The challenge was deferred when TWA encountered financial problems and was purchased by American Airlines. The terminal ended operations in October 2001, an early victim of the impact of 9/11 on air travel. Plans to encase the historic structure within a new terminal for JetBlue Airways triggered a revolt among preservationists; the National Trust for Historic Preservation and World Monuments Fund placed the terminal on their most endangered lists, drawing global attention to the threatened structure. In 2008 the Port Authority built a

Diffused lighting creates many shades of white in the ceramic-clad interior.

new crescent-shaped terminal for JetBlue Airways that partially wraps around the TWA facility and is connected to it by the original "flight tubes" that once led to the gate structures. Beyer Blinder Belle Architects & Planners undertook the restoration of the original terminal, and The Port Authority is working with a developer to repurpose the terminal as a hotel—allowing modern visitors to recapture, at least in part, the glamorous experience of early jet travel, and promising a happy ending for a landmark that almost became the Pennsylvania Station of the jet age.

There are no sharp corners in
the interior; even the stairs have
curved railings.

Solomon R. Guggenheim Museum

1959

1071 Fifth Avenue, Manhattan
Frank Lloyd Wright
Interior designated 1990

As visually compelling today as when it was built, Frank Lloyd Wright's celebrated and controversial spiral building contains an equally provocative interior, whose sweeping spiral ramp broke with all conventions of art museum design. Renovations and expansions to the building over the decades have not diminished the drama of the space, and its designation as a landmark (interior and exterior at the same time) was granted without opposition almost as soon as it was eligible.

The Guggenheim is one of only three projects Wright completed in New York—the others were an automobile showroom on Park Avenue (now demolished) and a prefab house on Staten Island—and he considered it his greatest achievement, calling it "My Pantheon." Though he had explored similar forms, beginning with his unbuilt reverse-spiral Automobile Objective of 1925, this is his first fully realized spiral interior.

Visiting the building is a unique experience, beginning with the approach. The pristine spiraling concrete exterior, formed of interlocking conical sections, has no visible windows and the revolving glass entrance doors are partly concealed. Inside, the low-ceilinged foyer opens dramatically onto a central six-story atrium, surrounded by a cantilevered ramp that ascends in gradually widening loops suggesting a nautilus shell and terminates in a spider web–patterned skylight dome.

The museum is designed to accommodate one thousand visitors at a time. Wright intended it to provide a continuous viewing experience, moving along a single path rather than from room to room, without retracing steps. The ramp begins at a lozenge-shaped fountain at the base of the atrium, opens into a first-level gallery, and continues upward, divided at intervals by partial concrete walls that create alcoves for paintings. The alcove walls are sloped, a feature that, Wright claimed, duplicated the angle of an easel. Separate galleries opening off the second and fourth levels provide more conventional museum-gallery viewing spaces.

Off-white walls and balustrades change tone with the varying illumination—natural light through the

From Picasso to Pollock

CLASSICS OF MODERN ART

From the ground level, the ramp coils upward in gradually widening loops. Along the way, equally spaced concrete ribs partition gallery alcoves.

The design achieves Wright's objective of creating a form of interpenetrating geometric shapes.

The skylight is the primary light source, supplemented by discreet indirect lighting.

skylight and narrow windows as well as concealed light fixtures. Beige terrazzo floors are inlaid with metal circles, echoing the form of the building. Other than occasional small planters, there is no ornamentation.

The museum was founded by businessman and philanthropist Solomon R. Guggenheim, whose art collection forms its core. He began collecting art in the 1890s, and under the guidance of painter Hilla Rebay, he acquired a collection of non-objective painting. Encouraging Guggenheim to build a museum to house it, Rebay recommended Frank Lloyd Wright, and in 1943 the seventy-six-year-old architect was given the commission. The design was completed by 1946, but went through many iterations, and construction was delayed by the uncertain postwar economy, the challenge of finding a builder for the unconventional structure, and then by Guggenheim's death in 1949. The foundation he had formed in 1937 passed to his nephew Harry F. Guggenheim, who undertook the execution of the project.

Wright died six months before the opening of the museum in October 1959. The interior garnered superlatives for its innovative design, though critics questioned its suitability for displaying art. Prominent artists protested that the building competed with the works exhibited, but the public responded en masse, with 750,000 visitors attending in the first nine months.

Over the ensuing years, the museum added to its collections and its activities, and parts of the original design were converted to other uses, including conservation and storage. A bookstore replaced the original drive-through loggia, and the restaurant became a conservation lab.

In 1988, just before it became eligible by age for landmark designation, the museum announced major expansion plans. Gwathmey Siegel & Associates designed an eight-story annex that stands as a backdrop to the original building and was designed along the lines of one proposed by Wright. The firm also supervised a three-year restoration of the interior that uncovered the skylight to bring natural light into the space, reclaimed exhibition areas that were being used for storage, and added a restaurant where the architect had originally intended one. In 2008 the exterior emerged from restoration with cracks filled and walls reinforced and repainted (in the color Wright had originally chosen).

Recognized as a unique example of convention-defying architecture, the Guggenheim came to symbolize New York as a center of avant-garde art. It was also a pioneering example of using architecture as a marketing tool and creating an art museum that is in itself an artwork, decades before the concept of museum-as-destination came into vogue.

Ford Foundation Building

1967

From 42nd Street, shallow brick stairs with brass railings lead into the atrium garden.

321 East 42nd Street, Manhattan
Kevin Roche John Dinkeloo and Associates
Dan Kiley, landscape architect
Interior designated 1997

Designated a landmark as soon as it became eligible, this is the most recent interior that the Landmarks Preservation Commission has protected to date. A radical departure from the glass curtain–walled rectangular skyscraper form pioneered in the Seagram Building, the Ford Foundation building is a twelve-story, block-wide rectilinear form of Cor-Ten steel–framed glass, the north and west sides of which form an L-shaped office section around a column-free, landscaped atrium that is more garden than interior.

Though its concept may be unique for a modern office building, the Ford Foundation follows the basic principles of the International Style as outlined by Henry-Russell Hitchcock and Philip Johnson in their 1932 book on the style: architecture as volume rather than mass, regularity rather than strict symmetry, and avoidance of applied ornament.

In the atrium, a densely planted garden ascends uphill in a succession of terraces from the 42nd Street entrance to the 43rd Street lobby. The rows of trees and foliage are an extravagant expanse of greenery in the center of the city. They create a cocoon of privacy within the open space, yet are visible from the street through the glass walls on the east and south sides of the building. Paths and steps of polished brick pavers run up and down the terraces through the lush garden. At its center is a square brick-framed pool. Pink-toned granite-clad corner piers emphasize the verticality of the atrium space, which rises 170 feet high and is crowned by a skylight formed of interlocking sawtooth members. Offices on two sides overlook the atrium, allowing employees to enjoy the garden and see one another, fostering a sense of community.

The project was one of the first commissions awarded to Roche and Dinkeloo, the surviving partners of Eero Saarinen, after they completed Saarinen's unfinished projects. Dan Kiley, another close Saarinen associate,

was responsible for the extensive and experimental planting scheme for the atrium, which included nearly forty trees, a thousand shrubs, and many thousands of vines and ground-cover plants.

On its completion, the Ford Foundation Building was hailed as an inspired example of modernist architecture and, according to *New York Times* critic Ada Louise Huxtable, "one of the most romantic environments ever devised by corporate man." Following its success, interior atriums have been enthusiastically adopted as amenities in countless modern buildings across the country, where they provide flattering contrast to steel-and-glass linearity. The building was also innovative in sustainable design, well before the concept became fashionable; carbon dioxide from the offices nourished the plants, which cleansed the air and produced oxygen that was recycled into the building's air-conditioning system.

The Ford Foundation was created in 1936 by automobile magnate Henry Ford and his son Edsel. In 1953 the foundation consolidated its headquarters in New York, initially in rented space. The idea of a self-sponsored building came from Henry Heald, who became president of the organization in 1956.

Heald had been president of the Illinois Institute of Technology, where he had overseen the construction of Mies van der Rohe's much-admired design of the campus, and he supported a similarly ambitious effort for the Ford Foundation. In 1963 the foundation purchased a Midtown property near Tudor City on which to build its headquarters. The site could have accommodated a far larger building with much more rentable space, but that was not the course Heald and the foundation chose to follow. With so few areas of respite in the busy metropolis, it was an extraordinary civic gesture, and one that presents unique preservation challenges.

Though the overall composition has been meticulously maintained, many of Kiley's original plantings unfortunately failed to thrive and were replaced with subtropical plantings better able to adapt to the temperate climate. Nevertheless, the Ford Foundation Building is an exceptional rendition of an architectural scheme that not only integrates interior and exterior but also embraces both modernity and nature.

The New Freedom in Design

Barbaralee Diamonstein-Spielvogel

In the last twenty-five years, good design, and its inspiration, has become readily available not only to design professionals, but also to the lay public and in many price ranges, almost everywhere in the United States. The field of interior design has evolved as an accessible creative outlet, and its prevalence has been accelerated by the increased exposure and familiarity with technology and a pervasive concern for the environment. Through reality television, the proliferation of style blogs, lifestyle publications, and social networking sites, residential, and even commercial, projects can be shared and critiqued. With the internet as an ever expanding platform, the expertise of interior designers is accessible to growing numbers of people. Interactive web applications offer many additional social networks, connecting clients with designers and architects. Other applications enable each of us to become our own interior designer, and to create—and design—a virtual prototype of any space. The possibilities for individual self-expression, particularly in defining one's own space, are almost limitless, and the freedom to design one's own surroundings is increasingly made visible as an indicator of one's perspective, personality, and a sometimes overheated barometer of our life and times.

This contemporary democratization of design is rooted in relatively recent history. A little over a century ago, interior design was not even considered a discipline. The publication in 1897 of *The Decoration of Houses* by Edith Wharton and Ogden Codman Jr. signaled the beginning of interior design as a genuine and respected area of study. The authors contended that decoration had, for too long, been merely the frequently unintentional accumulation of objects. Instead, they urged all to embrace the spatial proportion designated by a building's architecture, to design using common sense, and to value simplicity. This text led the way for the first generation of professional interior designers.

Much the way trends in design may be linked to society at large today, Wharton and Codman's manifesto reflected large-scale societal changes occurring in their time. The industrial revolution provided many with more leisure time and disposable income; industrialization made available opportunities never before seen, and women were gaining professional design prominence. A few of these women who advocated a "modern" sensibility in the home were Elsie de Wolfe, Ruby Ross Wood, and Syrie Maugham. None of the three had received any formal training in architecture, although they managed to carve out careers as prominent decorators.

Beginning in 1905, Elsie de Wolfe sought to contest the dreary functionalism of American decorating, which seemed centered around European period revivals and memorabilia. De Wolfe was the first to make interior design a "glamorous" pursuit; she introduced a model of "good taste" that still resonates today. Ruby Ross Wood emphasized the need for comfort as a governing principle of interior design, and Syrie Maugham assembled the first all-white rooms, as well as demonstrating a decidedly dramatic flair. These women all used their position in society, and their vibrant personalities, to influence life at home for many, carving out a role for interior design as a profession and discipline.

In the 1920s and 1930s, British decorators Vanessa Bell and Duncan Grant helped to revitalize the languishing decorative arts tradition in the United States by introducing original designs for murals, carpets, wallpaper, and furniture. In Europe, the Bauhaus integrated architecture, sculpture, painting, and the decorative arts into high-functioning ensembles. This introduction of industrial spatial formations and materials revolutionized residential design, and paved the way for modern design to be adopted in the United States. As the modern movement flourished, design became an increasingly deliberate and contemporary field, one that embraced technical skill with aesthetic sensibility. By the 1950s and 1960s "interior decoration" began to be known instead as "interior design," a shift in the lexicon that signaled a more expansive role for the discipline. Instead of just decorating with objects, interior designers became involved with the structural reorganization of a space.

If design is an indicator of our life and times, the increasing fluidity with which interior designers have assumed the roles of architect, furniture designer, and even lifestyle blogger speaks to the lack of a reigning paradigm. Today, a designer is not limited to one medium, but instead can, like Karim Rashid and John Saladino, move effortlessly from designing street signs and street furniture to creating prototypes for new kitchenware. Any and all objects have become the rightful purview of the designer. Similarly, a growing number of contemporary architects, such as Robert A.M. Stern, Richard Meier, and Rafael Vinoly have incorporated interior design into their projects, so that the interiors of their buildings are consonant with their exteriors. These developments suggest that we have entered a golden age of design, in which each object is important not only for its utility, but for its aesthetics as well. With this new appreciation for design, we can more deeply acknowledge the significant role of the designation of publicly accessible interior spaces by the New York City Landmarks Preservation Commission.

"Rescued, Restored, Reimagined" was developed by the New York School of Interior Design, one of the 139 diverse organizations that comprise the NYC Landmarks50

Alliance. This outstanding exhibition, which was part of the Alliance's efforts to commemorate the fiftieth anniversary of the passage of the NYC Landmarks Law, demonstrates clearly the contemporary relevance of interior landmark designations. We still treasure historic interiors because they reflect and speak directly to our imagination. An interior may please the eye, inform the mind, and educate us about the historical context of a building, while providing further commentary to better understand its time and period, and the people who inhabited it.

A visit to the kitchen in the 1832 Merchant's House is an education in the everyday challenges faced by people who cooked over an open hearth, while a visit to the rotunda in City Hall enables us to envision the grand aspirations of our early metropolis. With these designations, which include the Morris-Jumel Mansion, Radio City Music Hall, the Rainbow Room, and Four Seasons Restaurant, to name only a few, the commission has provided us with the ability to see how people in the past lived, worked, shopped, cooked, danced, drank, and slept. The designation of interiors enables us to more fully appreciate both the similarities and differences between the present and the past.

An interesting and perhaps unintended consequence of the designation of interior landmarks has been the strengthening of the crafts and trades on which earlier designs depended. The plasterwork that adorns a theater interior, the ornate grille of an Art Deco balustrade, the gilded metalwork or blown glass of a historic chandelier all require the often painstaking time, maintenance, and careful and educated hand of the gifted artisan. The revival and preservation of many of these crafts has sustained our thorough appreciation and respect for the often difficult but enduring methods of our forebears, who strove to create beauty and utility.

As we better comprehend, through our own efforts at creating our environments, the frequently difficult choices that one makes makes in color, style, and ornament, we can measure the divide between ourselves and the past. Sometimes that distance is great, but frequently it brings us closer together. To walk through the original interiors of a landmark and to see how others lived remains one of the most vital lessons in history for those with a sense of our past, and a vivid imagination.

All thanks to the New York School of Interior Design for this fitting tribute!

Interior Landmarks

Alvin Theater
1927
250 West 52nd Street, Manhattan
Herbert J. Krapp
Interior designated 1985

Ambassador Theater
1921
219 West 49th Street, Manhattan
Herbert J. Krapp
Interior designated 1985

American Museum of Natural History Memorial Hall, Theodore Roosevelt Memorial
1935
Central Park West between West 77th and West 81st Streets, Manhattan
John Russell Pope
Interior designer William Andrew Mackay
Interior designated 1975

American Telephone & Telegraph Company Building
1922
195 Broadway, Manhattan
William Welles Bosworth
Interior designated 2006

Apollo Theater
1914
253 West 125th Street, Manhattan
George Keister
Interior designated 1983

Appellate Division Courthouse
1899
27 Madison Avenue, Manhattan
James Brown Lord
Interior designated 1981

Barclay-Vesey Building
1927
140 West Street, Manhattan
Ralph Walker; McKenzie, Vorhees & Gmelin
Interior designated 1991

Barrymore Theater
1928
243 West 47th Street, Manhattan
Herbert J. Krapp
Interior designated 1987

Bartow-Pell Mansion Museum
1842
895 Shore Road, Pelham Bay Park, Bronx
Minard Lefever, Delano & Aldrich
Interior designated 1975

Beacon Theater
1929
2124 Broadway, Manhattan
Walter W. Ahlschlager, Rambusch Decorating Studios, Rapp & Rapp
Interior designated 1979

Belasco Theater
1907
111 West 44th Street, Manhattan
George Keister
Interior designated 1987

Biltmore Theater
1925
261 West 47th Street, Manhattan
Herbert J. Krapp
Interior designated 1987

Booth Theater
1913
222 West 45th Street, Manhattan
Henry B. Herts
Interior designated 1987

Bowery Savings Bank
1895
130 Bowery, Manhattan
McKim, Mead & White
Interior designated 1994

Bowery Savings Bank
1923
110 East 42nd Street, Manhattan
York & Sawyer
Interior designated 1996

Broadhurst Theater
1918
235 West 44th Street, Manhattan
Herbert J. Krapp
Interior designated 1987

Bronx General Post Office
1937
560 Grand Concourse, Bronx
Thomas Harlan Ellett
Interior designated 2013

Brooklyn Trust Company Building
1916
138 Pierrepont Street, Brooklyn
York & Sawyer
Interior designated 1996

Brooks Atkinson Theater
1926
256 West 47th Street, Manhattan
Herbert J. Krapp
Interior designated 1987

Central Savings Bank
1927
2100–2108 Broadway, Manhattan
York & Sawyer
Interior designated 1994

Chrysler Building
1930
405 Lexington Avenue, Manhattan
William Van Alen
Interior designated 1978

Cities Service Building
1932
70 Pine Street, Manhattan
Clinton & Russell, Holton & George
Interior designated 2011

City Hall
1811
City Hall Park, Manhattan
Joseph-François Mangin, John McComb Jr.
Interior designated 1976

Cort Theater
1912
138 West 48th Street, Manhattan
Thomas Lamb
Interior designated 1987

Crotona Play Center Bath House
1936
Fulton Avenue between East 172nd and East 173rd Streets, Bronx
Aymar Embury II
Interior designated 2007

Cunard Building
1921
25 Broadway, Manhattan
Benjamin Wistar Morris, Carrère & Hastings
Interior designated 1995

Daily News Building
1930
220 East 42nd Street, Manhattan
John M. Howells, Raymond M. Hood, J. Andre Fouilhoux
Interior designated 1998

Della Robbia Bar
1913
4 Park Avenue, Manhattan
Warren & Wetmore
Interior designated 1994

Dime Savings Bank
1908, 1918, 1932
9 DeKalb Avenue, Brooklyn
Mowbray & Uffinger (1908), Walker & Ward
(1918), McCormack & Helmer (1932)
Interior designer Adolph Alexander Weinman
Interior designated 1994

Dollar Savings Bank
1933
2526 Grand Concourse, Bronx
Halsey, McCormack & Helmer
Interior designated 1994

Ed Sullivan Theater
1927
1697 Broadway, Manhattan
Herbert J. Krapp
Interior designated 1988

Ellis Island, Main Building
1900
Ellis Island, Manhattan
Boring & Tilton
Interior designated 1993

Embassy Theater
1925
1560 Broadway, Manhattan
Thomas W. Lamb, Rambusch Studio
Interior designated 1987

Emigrant Industrial Savings Bank Building
1912
51 Chambers Street, Manhattan
Raymond F. Almirall
Interior designated 1985

Empire State Building
1931
350 Fifth Avenue, Manhattan
Shreve, Lamb & Harmon
Interior designated 1981

Eugene O'Neill Theater
1925
230 West 49th Street, Manhattan
Herbert J. Krapp
Interior designated 1987

Federal Hall National Memorial
1842
26 Wall Street, Manhattan
Town & Davis, John Frazee, Samuel Thompson,
William Ross
Interior designated 1975

Film Center Building
1929
630 Ninth Avenue, Manhattan
Ely Jacques Kahn
Interior designated 1982

Ford Foundation Bulding
1967
321 East 42nd Street, Manhattan
Kevin Roche John Dinkeloo and Associates
Dan Kiley, landscape architect
Interior designated 1997

Forty-Sixth Street Theater
1924
226 West 46th Street, Manhattan
Herbert J. Krapp
Interior designated 1987

Four Seasons Restaurant
1959
99 East 52nd Street, Manhattan
Philip Johnson
Interior designated 1989

Fred F. French Building
1927
551 Fifth Avenue, Manhattan
Sloan & Robertson, H. Douglas Ives
Interior designated 1986

Fuller Building
1929
41 East 57th Street, Manhattan
Walker & Gillette
Interior designated 1986

Gage & Tollner
1875
372 Fulton Street, Brooklyn
Designer unknown
Interior designated 1975

General Grant National Memorial
Riverside Park, Manhattan
John H. Duncan
Interior designated 1975

Goelet Building
1932
608 Fifth Avenue, Manhattan
Victor L. S. Hafner
Interior designated 1992

Golden Theater
1927
252 West 45th Street, Manhattan
Herbert J. Krapp
Interior designated 1987

Gould Memorial Library
1899
Hall of Fame Terrace at Sedgwick
Avenue, Bronx
McKim, Mead & White
Interior designated 1981

Grand Central Terminal
1913
89 East 42nd Street, Manhattan
Reed & Stem, Warren & Wetmore
Interior designated 1980

Greenwich Savings Bank
1922
Broadway and West 36th Street, Manhattan
York & Sawyer
Interior designated 1992

Hudson Theater
1904
141 West 44th Street, Manhattan
Israels & Harder
Interior designated 1987

Imperial Theater
1923
249 West 45th Street, Manhattan
Herbert J. Krapp
Interior designated 1987

**Interborough Rapid Transit System,
Underground Stations**
1904, 1908
Wall Street, Fulton Street, City Hall, Bleecker
Street, Astor Place, 33rd Street; 59th Street-
Columbus Circle, 72nd Street, 79th Street,
110th Street, 116th Street-Columbia U,
Manhattan; Borough Hall, Brooklyn
Heins & LaFarge
Interiors designated 1979

International Building
1935
630 Fifth Avenue, Manhattan
Associated Architects
Interior designated 1985

Jackie Robinson Play Center
1936
Bradhurst Avenue between West 145th and
153rd Streets, Manhattan
Aymar Embury II, Henry Ahrens
Interior Designated 2007

King Manor
1730
Jamaica Avenue and 150th Street, King Park,
Queens
Rufus King
Interior designated 1976

Lane Theater
1938
168 New Dorp Lane, Staten Island
John Eberson
Interior designated 1988

Little Theater
1912
238 West 44th Street, Manhattan
Ingalls & Hoffman, Ernest J. Krapp
Interior designated 1987

Loew's Paradise Theater
1929
2401–2419 Grand Concourse, Bronx
John Eberson, Beatrice Lamb
Interior designated 2006

**Long Distance Building, American
Telephone & Telegraph Company**
1914, 1916, 1932
32 Sixth Avenue, Manhattan
Cyrus Eidlitz (McKenzie, Voorhees & Gmelin),
Ralph Walker (Voorhees, Gmelin & Walker)
Interior designated 1991

Long Island Historical Society Building
1881
128 Pierrepont Street, Brooklyn
George B. Post
Interior designated 1982

Longacre Theater
1912
220 West 48th Street, Manhattan
Henry B. Herts
Interior designated 1987

Louis N. Jaffe Art Theater
1926
189 Second Avenue, Manhattan
Harrison G. Wiseman
Interior designated 1993

Low Memorial Library
1895
Columbia University
Broadway at West 116th Street, Manhattan
McKim, Mead & White
Interior designated 1981

Lyceum Theater
1903
149 West 45th Street, Manhattan
Herts & Tallant
Interior designated 1987

Madison Belmont Building
1925
181 Madison Avenue, Manhattan
Warren & Wetmore
Interior designated 2011

Majestic Theater
1927
245 West 44th Street, Manhattan
Herbert J. Krapp
Interior designated 1987

Manufacturers Trust Company Building
1954
510 Fifth Avenue, Manhattan
Gordon Bunshaft,Skidmore, Owings & Merrill
Interior designer Eleanor H. Le Maire
Interior designated 2011

Marine Air Terminal
1940
La Guardia Airport, Queens
Delano & Aldrich
Interior designated 1980

Mark Hellinger Theater
1929
237 West 51st Street, Manhattan
Thomas Lamb
Interior designated 1987

Martin Beck Theater
1924
302 West 45th Street, Manhattan
C. Albert Lansburgh
Interior designated 1987

The Metropolitan Museum of Art
1902
1000 Fifth Avenue, Manhattan
Richard Morris Hunt, Richard Howland Hunt,
consulting architect George B. Post
Interior designated 1977

Morris High School
1926
East 166th Street at Boston Road, Bronx
C. B. J. Snyder
Interior designated 1982

Morris-Jumel Mansion
1765
West 160th Street and Edgecombe
Avenue, Manhattan
Designer unknown
Interior designated 1975

Music Box Theater
1921
239 West 45th Street, Manhattan
C. Howard Krane, E. George Kiehler
Interior designated 1987

National City Bank Building
1841
55 Wall Street, Manhattan
Isaiah Rogers
Interior designated 1999

New Amsterdam Theater
1903
214 West 42nd Street, Manhattan
Herts & Tallant
Interior designated 1997

New School For Social Research Auditorium
1931
66 West 12th Street, Manhattan
Joseph Urban
Interior designated 1997

New York Central Building
1929
230 Park Avenue, Manhattan
Warren & Wetmore
Interior designated 1987

New York County Courthouse
1927
60 Centre Street, Manhattan
Guy Lowell
Interior Designated 1981

New York Life Insurance Building
1894
346 Broadway, Manhattan
Stephen Decatur Hatch; McKim,
Mead & White
Interior designated 1987

New York Public Library
1911
476 Fifth Avenue, Manhattan
Carrère & Hastings
Interior designated 1974

New York Savings Bank
1897
81 Eighth Avenue, Manhattan
R. H. Robertson
Interior designated 1988

Old Merchant's House
1832
29 East 4th Street, Manhattan
Designer unknown
Interior designated 1981

**Ottendorfer Branch, New York
Public Library**
1884
135 Second Avenue, Manhattan
William Schickel
Interior designated 1977

Palace Theater
1913
1564 Broadway, Manhattan
Kirchhoff & Rose
Interior designated 1987

Pierpont Morgan Library
1906
225 Madison Avenue, Manhattan
McKim, Mead & White
Interior designated 1982

The Plaza Hotel
1907, 1921, 1929
768 Fifth Avenue, Manhattan
Henry Janeway Hardenbergh, Warren &
Wetmore, Schultze & Weaver
Interior designated 2005

Plymouth Theater
1918
236 West 45th Street, Manhattan
Herbert J. Krapp
Interior designated 1987

Radio City Music Hall
1932
1260 Avenue of the Americas, Manhattan
Associated Architects, Edward Durell Stone
Interior designer Donald Deskey
Interior designated 1978

Rainbow Room
1934
30 Rockefeller Plaza, Manhattan
Associated Architects
Interior designer Elena Bachman Schmidt
Interior designated 2012

RCA Building
1931
30 Rockefeller Plaza, Manhattan
Associated Architects
Interior designated 1985

RKO Keith's Flushing Theater
1928
135-35 Northern Boulevard, Flushing, Queens
Thomas Lamb
Interior designated 1984

Royale Theater
1927
242 West 45th Street, Manhattan
Herbert J. Krapp
Interior designated 1987

**Sailors Snug Harbor, Chapel
and Building "C"**
1883, 1856
Richmond Terrace, Staten Island
Minard Lafever, James Solomon
Interior designer Charles Berry
Interior designated 1982

Scribner's Building
1913
597 Fifth Avenue, Manhattan
Ernest Flagg
Interior designated 1989

Seagram Building
1958
375 Park Avenue, Manhattan
Mies van der Rohe, Philip Johnson
Interior designated 1989

Seventh Regiment Armory
1881, 1911
643 Park Avenue, Manhattan
Charles W. Clinton, Robinson & Knust
Interior designated 1994

Shubert Theater
1913
225 West 44th Street, Manhattan
Henry B. Herts
Interior designated 1987

Solomon R. Guggenheim Museum
1959
1071 Fifth Avenue, Manhattan
Frank Lloyd Wright
Interior designated 1990

St. James Theater
1927
246 West 44th Street, Manhattan
Warren & Wetmore
Interior designated 1987

Steinway & Sons Reception Room
1925
109 West 57th Street, Manhattan
Warren & Wetmore
Interior designer Walter L. Hopkins
Interior designated 2013

Sunset Play Center Bath House
1936
7th Avenue at 43rd Street, Brooklyn
Herbert Magoon
Interior designated 2007

Surrogate's Court
1907
31 Chambers Street, Manhattan
John R. Thomas; Horgan & Slattery
Interior designated 1976

Time & Life Building
1960
1271 Avenue of the Americas, Manhattan
Harrison, Abramovitz & Harris
Interior designated 2002

**Tompkinsville (Joseph H. Lyons) Pool
Bath House**
1936
Victory Boulevard at Murray Hulbert
Avenue, Staten Island
Aymar Embury II
Interior designated 2008

Town Hall
1921
123 West 43rd Street, Manhattan
McKim, Mead & White
Interior designated 1978

Trans World Airlines Flight Center
1962
John F. Kennedy Airport, Queens
Eero Saarinen & Associates
Interior designated 1994

Tweed Courthouse
1881
52 Chambers Street, Manhattan
John Kellum, Leopold Eidlitz
Interior designated 1984

United States Custom House
1907
One Bowling Green, Manhattan
Cass Gilbert
Interior designated 1979

Van Cortlandt Mansion
1749
Broadway and West 242nd Street, Bronx
Frederick Van Cortlandt
Interior designated 1975

Walker Theater
1927
6401 18th Avenue, Brooklyn
Charles A. Sandbolm
Interior designated 1984

Western Union Building
1930
60 Hudson Street, Manhattan
Vorhees, Gmelin & Walker
Interior designated 1991

Williamsburgh Savings Bank
1875
175 Broadway, Brooklyn
George B. Post
Interior designated 1996

Williamsburgh Savings Bank
1929
1 Hanson Place, Brooklyn
Halsey, McCormack & Helmer
Interior designated 1996

Winter Garden Theater
1911
1634 Broadway, Manhattan
W. Albert Swasey
Interior designated 1988

Woolworth Building
1913
233 Broadway, Manhattan
Cass Gilbert
Interior designated 1983

Acknowledgments

This book was researched and written with the generous assistance of many pairs of helping hands, most of whom contributed their services. Contrary to the maxim, these contributing cooks added depth of flavor and seasoning to the broth, for which we are deeply grateful. Thanks to Elizabeth Battin, Alex Corey, Michael Munro, and Michael Hall for meticulous archival research, and to Michelle Scarola and Wes Horne for painstaking photo and permissions documentation. Janet Adams Strong contributed valuable insights into the significance and preservation history of the landmarks.

But the revelation of this book is the splendid color photography by Larry Lederman and the other talented photographers, which makes this a unique document bringing the spaces, materials, and details to life. We are grateful to Kitty Hawks for her support throughout the project and to John Maggiotto for his digital expertise.

At The Monacelli Press, Elizabeth White deftly steered the project through to publication, working with Michael Vagnetti. Designer Yve Ludwig has created a book as handsome as the interiors it celebrates. Finally, the New York School of Interior Design provided impetus and support for which we thank Board Chairman Dr. Patricia Sovern and President David Sprouls. And of course Barbaralee Diamonstein-Spielvogel, and her establishment of the NYC Landmarks50 Alliance, without which none of this would have happened.

Judith Gura and Kate Wood